2018

Merry
Christmas
Sweetheart ♡

I love you
M

HOLY WATERS

OF

Charleston

THE COMPELLING INFLUENCE OF
BISHOP JOHN ENGLAND
& FATHER JOSEPH L. O'BRIEN

W. THOMAS McQUEENEY

The
History
PRESS

Published by The History Press
Charleston, SC 29403
www.historypress.net

Front cover image, bottom: Courtesy of Ted Bobosh.

First published 2014

Manufactured in the United States

ISBN 978.1.62619.941.5

Library of Congress Control Number: 2014957349

CONTENTS

DEDICATION TO
BISHOP DAVID B. THOMPSON

It follows in sequence that the spiritual guidance and leadership of a diocese falls on the episcopate designated to the task. The propitious appointment of Bishop David B. Thompson as coadjutor bishop of Charleston in May 1989 brought a true pastoral dialogue to the Holy City. Like Bishop John England and Monsignor Joseph Laurence O'Brien, Bishop Thompson inventoried what was there to find out what was missing. For him, the chasm was evident. The timeliness of interfaith discourse was prioritized in an era when there were concerns of so much ambivalence in the secular world. Too many good young people were joining the legions of the un-churched. For this reason, Bishop Thompson planned a conference of statewide churches and synagogues. Discussions promoted a better understanding of religious importance and diversity in communities.

Energetic and determined, Bishop Thompson visited every parish in the diocese and returned often as his way of being personally available to all whom he could assist. His pastoral letter, "Our Heritage—Our Hope," initiated the Synod of Charleston, an official gathering of the Catholic community. The discourse was completed over nearly five years and did much to foster growth and to advance religious vocations.

It was under the leadership of Bishop Thompson that the move of Bishop England High School to the Daniel Island site was orchestrated in 1998. This process had begun in 1995 with the donation of forty acres from the Harry Frank Guggenheim Foundation. That construction

The eleventh bishop of Charleston, Right Reverend David B. Thompson. *Courtesy of Archival Office of the Diocese of Charleston.*

was one of many timely diocesan capital improvements made over the bishop's tenure.

Bishop Thompson, at seventy-five, stepped down from his role in 1999, as he had reached the age of mandatory retirement. Yet the Diocese of Charleston was further blessed with his devoted service for another fifteen years. His regular Sunday Mass at Christ Our King Parish was an inspiration for the worshippers. He crafted his brilliant three-point homilies to perfection. He did so without notes. He cited all who assisted, from the choir to the readers, Eucharistic ministers to the altar servers—by the warmth of friendship and sincere appreciation, always by their first names. His ingenuity, academic insights and incredible powers of recall were among his most charming personal traits, notwithstanding his constancy of humility and humor.

Though Bishop Thompson received many accolades during his decade-long pastorate, he was most humbled by the unexpected honor that reached into his remarkable interfaith friendships. The Tree of Life Award was presented to him as a result of his constancy in the promotion of interreligious harmony. The distinction represents the highest award given by the Jewish National Fund. As the eleventh bishop of Charleston, the meaningful presentation is most mindful of the inherent community strengths of Charleston's first bishop, John England.

Bishop Thompson passed away on November 24, 2013, at the age of ninety. It was through his friendship, guidance and insight that the production of this work was planned. It is to him, a man I deeply admired, that this work is dedicated.

W. THOMAS McQUEENEY

INTRODUCTION

S ometimes we look around and notice something important that should be celebrated, but nobody thought to send out the invitations. I acknowledged this in 2012 when the 200th anniversary of the War of 1812 rolled in and out of the calendar with barely a discernible yawn. Our South Carolina native son "Old Hickory" Andrew Jackson would be more than a bit dismayed. It was bad enough that he had engineered that war's most significant American victory, only to suffer the fact that it happened two weeks after the war had ended!

Understanding the dynamics of the world in which we live, it seems that everyone has a full schedule of other priorities—and so many of those are the sedentary urgencies imposed by electronic media. We have e-mailed, Tweeted and Facebooked our way into cyber-ambivalence. A daily dialogue with the keyboard-menacing masses has preempted one-on-one conversation with facial expressions, voice inflections and the pauses that emphasize introspective thought.

In my small world of Charleston, South Carolina, another celebration is in order, albeit one that would not be as ostentatious as warfare. My high school, where there may be students who are unaware of the major significance of its namesake, will be celebrating its 100th year. Bishop John England Memorial High School, as it was officially named, also represented a major step forward for Catholicity in South Carolina. I would not let this anniversary pass without homage to two Irish priests, one its namesake and the other its founder. They lived nearly a century apart but had so much in common that it inspired this effort.

With sincere thanks to the sharing of documents and information from the Diocese of Charleston archivist Brian Fahey, the generous donation of artifacts from the O'Brien family and the encouragement from the eleventh bishop of Charleston, Most Reverend David B. Thompson, the following pages are presented. I also benefited from the benevolence of the administration of Bishop England High School (BEHS) and the Marlene and Nathan Addlestone Library at the College of Charleston. Ironically, that library is situated on the former site of Bishop England High School (1922–98) and the Father O'Brien Gymnasium (1948–98). This is the school I attended for four years, from 1966 to 1970.

I had the good fortune of friendship with a special Irish couple, Eamonn and Karen Cassidy. Karen, a fine research historian, supplied support information that would be lost in the Atlantic Ocean otherwise. It seems that ocean had swallowed much of the John England family information over two centuries *trasna na dtonnta* (Gaelic for "across the seas"), as Karen noted. Karen supplied much genealogical information that had scarcely been associated with the England family on the shores west of Ireland.

I am grateful to Sister Anne Francis Campbell, archivist for the Sisters of Charity of Our Lady of Mercy, for allowing me access to relevant material in the congregation's archives and for sharing her knowledge of the life and times of Bishop England and Monsignor O'Brien.

My own personal interest in this subject was spurred by my father, who passed away in 2011. William T. McQueeney often spoke of his life's finest mentor, Monsignor Joseph Laurence O'Brien. Dad lost his mother as a teenager before World War II. His father was a disabled World War I veteran. He went to "Doc" O'Brien as an impressionable seventeen-year-old in dire circumstances with plans to join the war effort. He was given sound guidance and a holy blessing and handed a high school diploma in January of his junior year. The founder of Bishop England High School became my father's compass point, not only in his faith but also in his comportment of other areas of life. One of my eight siblings, Joseph Lawrence McQueeney, is named for Monsignor O'Brien.

My father was not alone. In my research, I have found so many other contemporary references to this great priest who died six days before I was born. His reach certainly remained beyond the span of his life.

Father O'Brien addressing those at a dedication of a church near his hometown of Avoca, Pennsylvania. *Courtesy of O'Brien family archives.*

Indeed, in speaking with three BEHS graduates—Walter V. Duane, Helen Dodds Shepherd and John LaTorre—I found that students were positively impacted over his long tenure as rector. "Doc" O'Brien built a lasting impression on countless students.

Duane, from the Bishop England class of 1939, gave firsthand testimony:

> *He would send us letters every month during the war* [World War II]. *It made you feel special that he cared. And he'd sign every one of them "Doc." It was his way of keeping you informed of the happenings in Charleston and at dear old Bishop England. If you were a B.E. graduate in the military service, you got a regular post from Doc. The art of letters has diminished over the generations, as has the energy and time it takes to show personal care and concern. Monsignor O'Brien was especially adept at remaining a part of each student's life well after high school.*

Walter V. Duane told of the universal admiration for Father O'Brien. *Photo by author.*

Shepherd of the class of 1945 concurred:

> *I was younger and was in the high school during the war. Father O'Brien was a true patriot and did so much to inspire and to boost the morale of those overseas fighting for freedom and our way of life. He was an extraordinary priest whom we all deeply admired. He was both a respected authority and a caring friend.*

"He changed my life," LaTorre confided.

From the class of 1948, LaTorre went off to college at the University of South Carolina to play football:

I confided in Doc that I had reached a point where I had made up my mind to drop out of college. In just a few days, I received a handwritten letter of encouragement from Doc convincing me that I needed to work hard and continue my education. That letter changed my life. I still have that letter as one of my most cherished possessions. I know he looked after a lot of people, but I always felt he took a special interest in me, and that's why I can never forget this amazing priest.

In preparing this work, it became clear that Monsignor O'Brien had studied Bishop John England in both an academic and a pastoral light. The 100th anniversary of the founding of the high school provided a reason for the study; the exuberance for the topic soon followed.

To properly celebrate this anniversary, it would be most beneficial to reestablish the significance of the name "John England." In doing so, I found a brave man who not only changed his home country but also brought his convictions to the American South. As in Ireland, his reputation and impact grew to proportions that exceeded his fifty-six years on earth. He was much studied and much admired in places well beyond his assigned three-state diocese.

Cenacle Sisters Convent postcard from 1906. This building served as Bishop England High School from 1916 to 1921. *Courtesy of May Forest Archives.*

Bishop England High School began in the old Cathedral School (known as the Pro Cathedral) in 1915 and then moved the following year to the building where the Cenacle Sisters once lived on Calhoun Street. The red brick enclave was completed on the adjoining lots in 1922. That school remained until 1998, when the high school was moved to a college-like campus on Daniel Island. The alumni include a most healthy share of scholars, priests and nuns, entrepreneurs, political figures, business leaders and others dedicated to the Catholic way of life. There are several families who now boast of a fourth generation of graduates. A monsignor's vision of a coeducational parochial high school found a niche that perhaps only he saw in 1914.

The year 1914, when Father O'Brien began planning to establish the new high school, had its other moments. It was the same year that Archduke Ferdinand was assassinated in Serbia, the kindling that lit World War I. The Panama Canal opened, shortening travel between the two great oceans. Owing to hostilities with Mexico, American marines occupied Vera Cruz. George Washington Carver, the son of a slave, began to revolutionize southern farming by virtue of his experiments with the peanut.

This effort is not so much for posterity as it is for the students and the parents of students, who may see that they have special opportunities because of two visionaries.

Topical and biographical research remains, perhaps, among the most tedious tasks necessary for every level of academia. The process of assembling the facts, the photographs and the letters of correspondence would—for me—also develop into interviews and even the reference of foreign travel. The travel was not for research but resulted in the reflection-connection of a resource. By my good fortune, I had been to Ireland nine times and to Cork City six times. Bandon (fifteen miles to the southwest) and Carlow (closer to Dublin) conjured the early years of Bishop England. St. Patrick College in Carlow had been founded near the time of England's birth and became a seminary exclusively for one hundred years. The college remains as an institution educating students in a spectrum of undergraduate programs and post-graduate law. Among its distinguished graduates are the "other famous" Catholic bishops, John Therry (first bishop of Australia), and Paul Cullen, the first Irish cardinal.[1]

I also traveled to Switzerland six times. It is a country of wondrous alpine scenery, much as I had dreamed to experience in my early geography lessons. Fribourg, where Joseph Laurence O'Brien studied at the old university, is less than twenty miles from Bern. Like St. Patrick in Carlow, the University of Fribourg remains a center of classical learning and academic research.

Other reference data was found. I gained new information from the archival files that the O'Brien family had kept and recently donated to the Diocese of Charleston. My friend Tom O'Brien handed the material to me personally. I carefully repaired old photographs digitally. Key quotes were rediscovered, such as Monsignor O'Brien's own words describing the choice of Bishop John England as the namesake for the new high school. We know that choice to be quite appropriate.

For the record, I loathe the tediousness of research like mostly everyone else, and I pre-apologize for the preponderance of the very necessary volume of endnotes. However, the more I delved into the subject, the more I found the need of the research—and the steering currents of the professionals who assisted me. As mentioned, they did so at great sacrifice of their own precious time.

Perhaps the sun rose upon an ocean view as John England looked home to Ireland. His commitment to administering to the sparse and wide flock of the early nineteenth-century American South propelled him to an endearment of scholars well beyond his lifetime. *Photo by author.*

Our modern world boasts of Generation X, the babies of the post–World War II Baby Boomers. Their children will likely have a different designation entirely. What this work purports to accomplish in its rediscovery of meaningful diocesan history and the accompanying biographical insights is to explain the foundational sense of the past before they become "Generation Who." They will, no doubt, find much more to every answer than my generation, as Baby Boomers, could have ever fathomed in innumerable questions. My generation diligently searched to find small bits of dated information by the Dewey Decimal System and the bleary-eyed reading of pertinent materials. The generation that reads this minor work will likely enjoy a deluge of information readily. Technologies will take them further than my imagination can comprehend.

We owe much to two gentlemen who lived a century apart. One was a newly consecrated Irish bishop for the recently created Diocese of Charleston, crossing the Atlantic to a new world of promise. Another was an Irish-American scholar from Pennsylvania who had earnestly studied the life of that same bishop before arriving in Charleston. Our waterfront welcomed both.

They have truly established the natural harbor we enjoy as holy waters.

Chapter 1

BRETHREN OF RISK

Bishop John England and his biographer, Monsignor Joseph Laurence "Doc" O'Brien, were risk-takers who shared much more than their Irish heritage. They not only changed Catholicity in Charleston but also furthered the acceptance of the previously downtrodden Catholics statewide.

All religions were guaranteed freedoms by the John Locke "Fundamental Constitutions of Carolina."[2] Well, almost. That constitution was never ratified by the assembly but did have the shadow of religious freedom, inviting Jews, Lutherans, Quakers and others to the gifted land. Owing to European conflict, Catholics were not as welcome. Though the American Revolution expanded freedoms, that expansion was not extended to all citizens. Slavery existed. And the shadow of religious bias existed as well.

The new times of Catholic enterprise brought just the right man to the southern harbor that the sea currents washed into destiny—Charleston. The early twentieth century produced another priest to be a catalyst of faith building in the harbor of learning. They were somewhat the same cleric, only separated by a century. Their one kindred calling uplifted many a searching soul, regardless of religious affiliation. They each left the known comforts of their respective families.

Risk was a given in most ways of American life in the times of these two priests. There was the robust risk of sickness; cholera, malaria, tuberculosis and yellow fever were ever present in both centuries.

Bishop John England. The original portrait remains in the Diocesan Archives of Charleston, South Carolina.

Neither priest had the early advantage of vaccinations that had changed life expectancy, from Alexander Fleming's penicillin (1928) for infectious disease to Dr. Jonas Salk's polio prevention (1953). Other risk was evident by the stream of constant human conflict—

wars and political upheavals that ravaged generations of youth across the world. Bishop England experienced the Irish rebellion of 1798, its failure sending his own father into hiding for a year.[3] Father O'Brien saw the greatest conflicts of modern civilization—World Wars I and II. Both England and O'Brien had known the disasters of famine

Monsignor Joseph Laurence O'Brien. *Courtesy of O'Brien family archives.*

(the Irish crop failures of the early nineteenth century and the crop failures of America's Great Depression in the 1930s). Charleston was built for risk, owing to the devastation expected from the great storms that marched across the mid-Atlantic Ocean every other decade. A hurricane was never a surprise to a Charlestonian.

A citizen of Charleston would expect risk as much as one would expect justice, commerce and societal interaction. But all were treated in the heartbeat of life—with varying degrees of impact. When Bishop England arrived, the societal risks were evident—an economy based on slavery and religious toleration evident in theory but not in practice. When Father O'Brien came from Pennsylvania, he was met with a strong southern predisposition of distrust of Yankee oversight. There remained veterans of the Confederate States of America scattered about Charleston in 1914, barely fifty years after the cessation of North-South hostilities. He knew the risk. Both priests had the added difficulty of inadequate funding.

Risk begets reward, especially when the diligence of purpose is cemented.

The coast of Ireland near Cobh, formerly Queenstown, a point of departure for newly consecrated Bishop John England in 1820. *Photo by author.*

The Compelling Influence of Bishop John England & Father Joseph L. O'Brien

Both Bishop England and Monsignor O'Brien left a legacy of that dedication, showing an industrious and energetic spirit with an overcrowded résumé for a singular lifetime. They "lived wide." The summaries of their individual accomplishments filled pages. Those being citations of greatness, it was not what they had each intended. They took risks to gain the value of progressive significance. They each donated their expertise, their energy and their existence to causes greater than themselves. They benefited innumerable others in the form of leadership, learning and lasting institutions. They bolstered faith. Their separate legacies remain as exemplary lives based within considerable selfless aspects.

It is the spirit of discovery and rediscovery of what two gentleman priests have borne and bequeathed that underscores their tolerance of risk in a world riddled with its debris. Fear of failure could be its own catalyst. It is certainly a better condition than the more available reason—fear of effort.

Chapter 2

CATHOLIC BEGINNINGS IN THE AMERICAN SOUTH

In order to bring the young Bishop John England to the new three-state Diocese of Charleston, it would be useful to set the existing stage of Catholicism in the American South, and especially in Charleston. By the bishop's own calculations, there were only 7,500 Catholics in all of South Carolina—and fewer in the adjoining states. Only 500 lived in North Carolina and about 3,000 in Georgia.[4] The European nationalities that had delivered this Catholic population were mostly French and Irish. Both were newly arrived, owing to incidents elsewhere. The French came from two specific events: an uprising in Santo Domingo (known historically as the 1791 Haitian revolution) and the French revolution (1789). The Irish who came were from yet another attempted revolution, set in 1798, and modeled after the American Revolution of 1776. Its short duration and failure made an escape from Ireland necessary for Catholics who were part of the Society of United Irishmen.[5] America had the promise of religious freedom that gave each group a new start in a country of much promise.

It is historically evident that John Locke's *Fundamental Constitutions of Carolina* provided the impetus of religious freedom and was a major source work for the United States Constitution. Jews, Quakers and the French Huguenots came to Charles Towne (renamed "Charleston" after the American Revolution). Catholics were in another category. Restrictive British law had previously prevented parishes in the

St. Mary's was the first Catholic parish in the Carolinas and Georgia (1789). The rebuilt church dates to 1838. *Photo by author.*

Carolinas. Why? There was a societal attitude that "from the sixteenth century, Englishmen pictured the Roman Church not merely as a system of cruelty and intolerance, but as an international conspiracy operating through secret agents and with the covert sympathy of fellow travellers."[6] These awkward beliefs from the Protestant-dominated society of young America prevailed in the mindset of the new nation— even though the rights of man, tolerance and freedom were being championed. Indeed, after the Revolution, religious acceptance often drifted to old-world divides—gaps betraying the intention of the U.S. Constitution's First Amendment.

As a British colony, the dominant churches were the Church of England (Episcopal) and the Church of Scotland (Presbyterian). The emancipation from British rule with the Treaty of Paris (1783) meant that the French and Irish were no longer coming to a British world but, rather, to a world of unbridled freedoms. Nonetheless, Catholics remained in a lower level of citizenship due to the extant and lingering British customs. In many quarters, the Papists were despised by association to factions in almost every old-world connotation—with the warring Spanish, the aristocratic French and the subjugated Irish Catholics.

The French Catholics were in need of a congregational assembly. They rented and then purchased a house and lot on Hasell Street (1788) and formed the Church of St. Mary (August 1789).[7] The Irish Catholics were part of their early membership but were robust in their growth. The French incorporated the conformity they practiced in the West Indies to appoint a council of church oversight—a vestry, much akin to the practices of the Episcopal faith.

The first three priests of the congregation were Irish: Father Matthew Ryan, Father Thomas Keating and Father Simon Felix Gallagher. Through expectations of traditional Vatican allegiance, the lay trustees of St. Mary's (the vestry) struggled with the friction of pastoral authority. The early abiding authority remained with the vestry. Later, "at a vestry meeting on March 26th, 1810 a resolution was passed to appoint a committee to draw up new rules for the future government of the church."[8] That resolution denied the vote or presence of the pastor at vestry meetings. Talk about a puzzling disconnect! The powerful vestry had excluded the parish priest. That vestry was composed of a cross section of parishioners, though most, by 1810, were of Irish birth or Irish descent.[9]

By 1816, it became apparent that the vestry of St. Mary's and the archbishop of Baltimore, who had full oversight, were to remain at odds. Concurrently, in Ireland, the events that led to Father England's elevation were in progress. The contemporaneous timing was, in fact, related.

In 1817, Father England resigned his trusteeship with the Chronicle *and accepted a pastorship of the church of Bandon, a town about sixteen miles southwest of Cork City. While the young pastor was devoting himself to his new duties, schism was racking the Church in faraway Charleston, South Carolina. As the particulars involve a long and complicated story, suffice it to say that lay trusteeism and rampant nationalism had combined to produce the scandalous situation. Put simply, the schism occurred in 1816 when the lay trustees of Saint Mary's, the only Catholic congregation in Charleston, refused to accept as their pastor the French-born Father J.P. DeCloriviere appointed by the Archbishop of Baltimore. The Archbishop placed Saint Mary's under interdict. Father DeCloriviere then opened a chapel on Cannon Street and Ashley Avenue for the members of the congregation willing to submit to the Archbishop's authority. Matters came to a head in 1819 when the schismatics promoted a scheme to establish an Independent Catholic Church with an Irish priest consecrated by the Jansenist Bishop of Utrecht as its head. The Archbishop of Baltimore, the Most Reverend Ambrose Marechal dispatched Father Benedict Fenwick, S.J., the future Bishop of Boston, to Charleston to remove the interdict as soon as the trustees would submit to authority. Father Fenwick managed to restore some semblance of peace and unity, yet the attempt to form an Independent Church convinced Rome that something had to be done. Acting upon Archbishop Marechal's suggestion, the Sacred Congregation of Propaganda decided to detach the Carolinas and Georgia from the Archdiocese of Baltimore and form them into a new Diocese with the Bishop's residence in Charleston. In June, 1820, having studied the problem for a year, the Sacred Congregation recommended and Pope Pius VII approved the erection of the See of Charleston with John England as its first Bishop.*[10]

The trustee system became a common practice in the new United States, since religious entities were not allowed to own property. Monsignor Joseph Laurence O'Brien's 1934 publication, *John England: The Apostle to Democracy*, explains this dynamic.

American Catholic Church history has been marred much more by the specter than the reality of Trusteeism, which ever since has been used by the bishops as a club to keep the laity in submission. The laws of the new nation required that church property be placed in the possession of a lay corporation; in the early American Catholic churches this corporation was known as the trustees, and it operated much as was already the case in French Canada at that time. For the great majority of cases this system worked very well, but in a small minority of cases, partly because of manipulative Irish priests and partly because of some poor administrative tactics by several bishops, cases of serious open conflict between the bishop and the trustees of certain churches developed—in one case a young lawyer named Abraham Lincoln defended the trustees. Because of their notoriety these few cases attained more importance than they intrinsically merited, and the fumbling of the bishops only tended to exacerbate the problems.

Charleston of 1820 was the scene of one of the longest and most bitter of these trustee conflicts. One might have expected that the situation might

have forced a vigorous young bishop from outside the United States to make authoritative kinds of moves. Nothing, however, could have been farther from the truth with Bishop John England. His initial and subsequent actions were the very epitome of toleration, democracy and voluntarism. For England, the evils of Trusteeism were the result of the failure of proper constitutional provisions in the original trustee charters. England responded to the sources of these evils by creating his constitutional form of government.[11]

Father Clorivière (top) and Father Fenwick (as bishop of Boston). *Courtesy of National Archives.*

In the few years leading to the establishment of the Charleston Diocese, the first archdiocese of the United States was established in Baltimore. John Carroll (1735–1815) was consecrated as the first United States archbishop. Archbishop Carroll was the cousin of Charles Carroll of Carrollton, the only Catholic to sign the Declaration of Independence. After Archbishop Carroll's passing, his successor, Archbishop Leonard Neale, had an abbreviated tenure, dying in 1817. The French immigrant Archbishop Ambrose Maréchal followed.

Joseph-Pierre Picot de Limoëlan de Clorivière (1768–1826), the priest who had to move to Cannon Street, would warrant a full study separate of this work. The priest whom St. Mary's parish would not accept had an interesting pre-ordination résumé. He was an adventurer, a successful businessman and an accomplished artist and was the only man to escape an assassination attempt on Napoleon's life. Some of his miniature portraits are presently displayed in Charleston's Gibbes Museum of Art.

Another person of historic interest emerged from the early schismatic times to the authority of John England. Father Simon Felix Gallagher, the third pastor of St. Mary's, was one of the eight founders of the Hibernian Society of Charleston (formed 1799, chartered 1801). He became the first president of that society, the oldest benevolent Irish society in America. Father Gallagher was a dichotomy. His influence on the early Catholic congregation was substantial, and he later became the most notable obstacle to the church hierarchy's restoration of order.

It was because of the efforts of Jesuit Father Benedict Fenwick that Bishop England could begin his 1821 tenure in Charleston without the impediments of St. Mary's lay vestry. Within thirteen months, the issue had been resolved, and this landmark church and assembly graduated to the affairs of traditional canon law.

Father Fenwick met the ship that carried Bishop John England from Ireland. The new bishop was quickly apprised of all matters and began his duties in humble service to all that he had inherited in the three-state diocese. His perceptive handling of the still-smoldering schism gave insight to his ability to gain the confidence of Catholics and, eventually, the entire community.

> *Bishop England's first response to the challenge of schism was both peaceful and wise. Giving not the least hint of anger or revenge, he took no legal action and imposed no church penalties on the troublemakers…He quietly negotiated a three-year lease of St. Mary's Church from the trustees, rather than making himself their hostage by using a church they controlled. At the same time, he arranged for the construction of another church, which could be designated as Charleston's Cathedral. He did what he had been ordained to do: he watched over and ministered to the people as their priest. Before long, the great majority of Charleston's Catholic community found themselves touched by the openness and kindness of their new bishop. They recognized in him a true spiritual shepherd, and they followed his lead. The trustees, for the most part, were left talking to themselves.*

[Father] *Gallagher departed for Florida with England's blessing.*
Arranging a full reconciliation with the stubborn trustees would take
more time and considerable patience on the part of the new bishop. It
was already clear, however, that he had won the contest in Charleston.
And he had done it as a man of peace.[12]

In his diary that he kept since 1821, Bishop England expressed the
concern of losing good Catholic parishioners over the politics of church
authority. His concern was that they would become Methodists, who
were aggressive in their recruitment at the time.[13]

The bishop had broader activities to attend. Catholics in a three-state
diocese needed the full benefit of the Sacraments. It was important to
travel to the remote regions and to celebrate Mass within myriad venues
that were not Catholic churches.

Charleston was once a walled city—the only British walled city in
North America. The walls came down in due course once the British
ruled the seas. The city itself became among the most affluential in the
Western Hemisphere. By 1790, it boasted the fourth largest population in
the former colonies, only trailing New York, Philadelphia and Boston.[14]
By Bishop England's arrival, it was sixth, surpassed by Baltimore and

A postcard depicting the newly built Cathedral of St. John the Baptist, circa 1906.
Courtesy of May Forest Archives.

New Orleans (which had not been a U.S. city in 1790). There was wealth. There was optimism. There was growth. John England had arrived at a place where the exuberance of a burgeoning America was still evident but where the Catholic Church was mired in the status of a mission effort. He recognized the work to be done.

One could postulate that, given the foundation of religious freedom and the exposure to world trade, Charleston was destined to become a fine port welcoming all faiths. But that was not the case upon England's arrival. It took the right man at the correct time. Fate played remarkable music in the small ensemble of Catholic beginnings in the Holy City.

St. Mary's Church became an important bastion of Catholicity in the Carolinas for the next two hundred years. The second Charleston church, St. Finbar's—built near Broad and Legare Streets—initiated another foundation of worshippers. St. Finbar's possessed the added advantage of a man considered among the greatest orators of his time: Bishop John England.

Part of St. Finbar's eventual reconstruction as the Cathedral of St. John the Baptist houses the vault that is graced with John England's remains. Symbolically, the cathedral was built upon John England's work. In a larger sense, Catholicism in the Carolinas and Georgia would point to this man as its spiritual foundation.

Chapter 3

ENGLAND'S IRELAND

B ishop John England, accompanied by his sister Joanna and Father Denis Corkery, arrived in Charleston from Ireland on December 30, 1820. He traveled to Charleston aboard the ship *Thomas Gelston*.[15] He championed the American way of life in his oratory. Freedom mattered. In Ireland, there was no such fulfillment for Catholics under the stringency of British rule.

Timing was favorable for the young John England. Through a full century of excruciating Penal Codes, the Irish had precious few rights. A timely repeal of some of the codes (from 1778 to 1793) advanced John England's opportunities. It was not until 1778 that the codes even allowed a Catholic to marry a Protestant. By that same year, a ban on some of the codes allowed the Irish to lease land. Though the difficulties were lessening in the late eighteenth century, the British-Irish conflicts continued into recent times.[16]

England was born in 1786, the first of ten children.[17] His natural thirst for knowledge propelled him. His family had weathered the failed Irish Rebellion of 1798 when John was only fourteen. They were certainly familiar with the strife of the era.

John England's family had suffered under the tyranny of the anti-Catholic Penal Codes. His grandfather had been imprisoned for four years, and his father, threatened with transportation to the West Indies for the terrible crime of teaching school, had spent a year hiding in the mountains of County Cork.[18]

Right: Gates of the Green Coat School in Cork, previously only available to Protestants. *Courtesy of Karen Cassidy*.

Below: St. Patrick's College, Maynooth, County Carlow, Ireland. *Courtesy of Karen Cassidy*.

One early penal law (repealed by a law of 1782) disallowed an Irishman to gain an education at a Protestant school. England was able to attend the Green Coat School, which had previously been an all-Protestant institution for young boys. This was the first of several ameliorations of Irish law that had great benefit to his generation.

With intentions to enter the legal profession, England spent two years studying law, also recently allowed by a recent repeal. His later diary speaks to these times and his decision to enter the Seminary of St. Patrick at Carlow. He was only seventeen. He was torn between the need for Irish political leadership and the dedication of his life to religious orders. As his life evolved, he actually was able to perform both functions simultaneously.

England had studied the model of American democracy and had adopted America in his mind and heart well before he crossed the Atlantic. He committed the words "inalienable rights" that changed the world from classist ideology to the rights of every man. The American Declaration of Independence was to him the embodiment of timely secular freedoms established as a model for the world. He printed words of the First Amendment of the United States Constitution as a banner above his later landmark American publication, *The United States Catholic Miscellany*: "Congress shall make no law respecting an establishment of religion, or prohibiting the free exercise thereof."

England saw the expressions of freedom as something that could flourish in the minds of like-minded people. But he had the old-world contentiousness to confront in Ireland. His constant editorial challenge to the British restrictions, in view of ever-present retribution, made him a passionate leader in the eyes of his readership. England had gained a similar following for his oratory. He became a vehement advocate for change to improve the Irish condition.

> *The young man had a great way with his pen, and his oratory, mixing a tradesman's common sense with romantic, dramatic images worthy of a poet, moved audiences, Protestant and Catholic alike, at least to sympathy if not to a singleness of opinion. He was a patriot through and through, republican in politics and Gallican in religion.* [19]

His ordination to the priesthood on October 11, 1808, formalized his commitment to serve Christ and the Catholic Church. In Cork, he was instrumental in the administration of several local charitable and educational institutions. He attended to an asylum, to the Cork jail and to the soldiers at the Cork garrison.[20] By 1812, he began teaching theology at the College of St. Mary. By 1814, England published a monthly

Father John England served as pastor at the North Presentation Convent and Church. His younger sister, Mary, as Sister Catherine, joined this convent. *Courtesy of Karen Cassidy*.

newsletter, the *Religious Repository*, and helped guide the larger *Cork Mercantile Chronicle* to a wider readership, being its featured columnist.[21] His influence grew.

An attestation of his effectiveness as both a Catholic priest and an important Irish leader of his generation developed from his assignment to the Bandon Church, near Cork. The famed gates of Bandon contained the warning "Turk, Jew or Atheist may enter here, but not a Papist."[22] England was not welcome. In spite of the decided bigotry and abhorrent warning, the young priest's oratorical skills soon won over many of the townsmen of every political and religious persuasion. He became accepted in a most difficult setting—Bandon. No previous Catholic priest had attempted or achieved prominence there.

Bandon had been developed as a walled town more than a century earlier and had been chartered as a Protestant-only community. Given the times, the infamous main gate still stood upon John England's arrival. Yet even the Bandon community embraced Father England.

England had proven to be a student of democracy and nonviolent disagreement. He came to be admired for his elocution of pertinent socio-political matters.

Even with his considerable skills, Father John England could never appease the ruling British. Timely orders soon came from Rome in June 1820. Archbishop Ambrose Marèchal, by way of pastoral need in the fledgling United States, had recommended the creation of the Diocese of Charleston. Pope Pius VII appointed Father England to become the first bishop to serve the newly formed diocese. Upon this elevation and ordination, the new bishop refused the customary allegiance to the British Crown, only reserving allegiance to the papacy in Rome. This egregious omission was met with rancor from the Protestant authorities who heretofore had demanded allegiance to the British Crown for each ordained bishop. England noted to the informed authorities that he would make proper allegiance to his newly chosen country, America, and left in a matter of months for Charleston. The new diocese encompassed the states of North and South Carolina, as well as Georgia. His departure certainly diffused much more than religious and political fervor he would have supported by remaining in Ireland. It also separated him from his most vehement ally, the Irish patriot Daniel O'Connell.

England left for Charleston just six years after the signing of the Treaty of Ghent (1814), the official cessation of the second war of American independence fought against the British. The Irish had their own tussle with the British, dating back centuries. And the British had no affinity for the newly ordained Bishop John England, once described as an irritant to the Crown "only exceeded by the Irish Liberator, Daniel O'Connell."[23] But O'Connell remained.

Indeed, Daniel O'Connell and John England had much in common. Both were contemporaneous graduates of St. Patrick College in Carlow, Ireland. They had become like-thinking friends. Both were outspoken leaders extolling the determination of an independent Catholic Ireland. Both believed in nonviolent means to reach accord. Both were celebrated orators, well known for their ability to humor and inspire. Both died away from their beloved Ireland—O'Connell on the way to Rome at Genoa, and England in Charleston.[24] Daniel O'Connell certainly missed the wit and pen of John England. The Irish patriot lives on. In Ireland's capital of Dublin, he is quite evident. The main thoroughfare and the major bridge across the River Liffey are both named for O'Connell. Along the route, one would find an enormous statue of the same rebellious associate of Father England— Mr. Daniel O'Connell. The two, England and O'Connell, were giants of the Irish cause and are forever linked to their times.

Those in Charleston had no idea of the strength of character England had postured against the ruling British in Cork. Much of what came forward as his early homeland contributions to the cause of Irish independence arrived as information well after England's death, since England was loath to extol the merits of his past. His experiences in Ireland, undisputedly, gave noble argument to injustices he encountered in America, most notably in the condition of black slavery. He had experienced the injustices of one society enforcing a will upon another in Ireland. This would give him a mindset for seeking solutions and repair in America. He left for America quite aware of the inconsistencies but encouraged by the greatest civil promise of its age: the Constitution of the United States.

As England brought a younger sister, Joanna, with him to Charleston, the other eight siblings remained in Ireland. His brother Thomas and sister Mary (as Sister Catherine) devoted their lives to religious orders. Two of John England's nephews remained and led impactful lives in Ireland. These first cousins were also named for their uncles: John England, professor of physics and natural philosophy at Queens College (now known as University College Cork), and Thomas England, who became the parish priest at Killavullen in North Cork. At Killavullen Church, there remains a monument to Father Thomas England inscribed as follows:

But land or deck on
You may safely reckon,
Whatsoever country
You come hither from,
On an invitation
To a jollification
With a parish priest
That's called "Father Tom"

The England family in Ireland and abroad rose from the status of noteworthy to the level of "most significant." The bishop was an exemplary family leader who represented a quite exemplary family. The

England legacy remains in the home country of Ireland; those in Cork are well aware of this extraordinary prelate and the benefit that Ireland continued to receive from his relatives who remained.

John England's Ireland and his America were both beset by prejudices. There were great divides. The eloquence he exhibited as a young priest in both written word and oratory in his native Ireland set a fine foundation for his impassioned following in America.

Chapter 4

UPON THE PIER OF THE HOLY CITY

Decembers are sometimes balmy in Charleston—a weather condition not likely in wintertime Cork. Like the weather patterns, England hoped to find the temperature of his new home warmed by optimism and welcome. Reverend Benedict Fenwick, SJ, met England at the pier on the last Sunday of 1820.

Bishop England's new responsibility had many challenges in the new diocese. To be sure, he came from a Catholic country controlled by Protestants. The young bishop, only thirty-four, arrived at a Protestant country slightly more tolerant of Catholics but still not to the point of equality. The secular freedoms, Bishop England must have concluded, were well worth the new experiment of democracy. He had been challenged and had done much in the quest to improve Ireland's plight. Charleston was a new beginning.

What he accomplished as Charleston's bishop was extraordinary. It was from his enlightenment, his conviction and his exuberance for his new country that he achieved so very much past the stretch of two decades.

Bishop John England had many priorities when he arrived in Charleston in 1820. He founded a Catholic newspaper, The United States Catholic Miscellany; *he established the cathedral church, St. Finbar; he opened the Seminary of St. John the Baptist to train native clergy; he dispatched what priests he had to minister to the surrounding plantations; and he founded an order of women religious, the Sisters of Charity of Our Lady of Mercy.*[25]

A typical Irish transport ship, the *Jennie Johnston*, circa 1820. *Painting by author.*

The entrance scene to May Forest Motherhouse, home of the Sisters of Charity of Our Lady of Mercy, founded by Bishop John England in 1829. *Photo by author.*

Bishop England became a very busy leader administering a foundation of institutions needed to find Catholics, two centuries hence, established and comfortable in the profession of faith. It was not always so!

The new bishop arrived to face newer and different prejudices than he had left in Cork. No bias could have exceeded the centuries-long British disdain for Catholicism and the Irish in general. Through those Penal Codes, famines and other atrocities, the Irish were beaten down. Many had left. Indeed, in the decade between 1845 and 1855, 1.8 million Irish left the home country for other lands.[26] To stay was to face deprivation.

Bishop England, as the exceptional orator, developed a following that grew once he had arrived in Charleston. Many who enjoyed his abilities and insights were not Catholic. The respect he had gained certainly arrested much early nineteenth-century anti-Catholic fervor. His travels underscored his resolve and ability to relate to the common man.

> *England liked to exploit the apparent contradiction between his ecclesiastic rank and his advocacy of republican equality. On one of his many diocesan tours through Georgia and both Carolinas, he visited the remote village of Columbus, which was separated from Savannah by three hundred miles of dusty, sweaty travel in a horse-drawn jingle. As few Catholics of substance lived in the town, England had made reservations at what passed as a hotel. The townsfolk, all Protestant, eagerly crowded the lobby and waited for the strange creature to arrive. Finally, someone—surely not a Catholic bishop?—a middle-sized man, covered in road dust and sun-burnt, drew his two spent horses to a stop outside the hotel. He jumped down, strode into the lobby, "stripped off his coat, hat, and vest; washed his face and hands," and demanded a good glass of wine, which he drank down heartily. The crowd studied his every gesture. Only when the glass was dry did he produce a "large and lustrous" ring from his pocket, and, "with his jeweled hand," sign his name to the register, John Bishop of Charleston. No doubt he meant to astonish the crowd, which was duly astonished.[27]*

He took risks others would not dare, based on the words in that U.S. Constitution he had studied in Ireland. One risk was to assist the needs of those brought from the African continent as slaves.

> *Combating hostility to the faith, winning converts, and ministering to his small flock of black and white Catholics thoroughly occupied Bishop*

England. In the summer of 1835 he opened a school for free blacks in Charleston. Taught by two seminarians and two nuns, the school enrolled eighty students within a few weeks. Pro slavery Charlestonians, however, vehemently opposed the opening of this landmark school. England saw the situation as a threat to Catholics as well as to blacks. After a two-day standoff, he reluctantly agreed to close the school on condition that all religious schools for free blacks close as well as his Catholic school. [28]

Bishop England reopened the school in 1841.

He had left a country that facilitated an authoritative society imposing unjust rule on one that was subordinated, though conditions were not as oppressive as the practice of slavery. Nonetheless, human rights were at risk for a class of people in Ireland. These same rights were trampled upon in young America. He predicted its resolution: "Slavery, it is true, continues amongst us, and whatever may be the opinions and desires of the South upon the subject, it is impossible that it should be abolished for a considerable time to come without the most injurious results, not merely to property, but to society." [29]

England's intellectual discourse was ahead of its time and much ahead of the vehement results the South would suffer within three decades of his prophecy.

A striking phase of Bishop England's apostolic character was manifested in his spiritual care of the negroes. He celebrated an early Mass in the Cathedral for them every Sunday and preached to them at this Mass and at a Vesper service. He was accustomed to deliver two afternoon sermons; if unable to deliver both, he would disappoint the rich and cultured who flocked to hear him, and preach to the poor ignorant Africans. [30]

His dedication to the needs of others precluded his own. He was an exemplary attestation to the Christ-like ideals often seen in the lives of past Catholic saints. He had no pretensions other than to lead by word, action and prayerful sacrifice.

In the epidemics of those days he exhibited great devotion to the sick, while his priests and the Sisters of Mercy volunteered their services in the visitations of cholera and yellow fever. His personal poverty was pitiable. He was known to have walked the streets of Charleston with the bare soles of his feet to the ground. Several times the excessive fatigue and exposure incurred in his visitations and ministrations prostrated him, and more than once he was in danger of death. Twice he visited Haiti as Apostolic Delegate. In 1823 he was asked to take charge of East Florida and, having been given the powers of vicar-general, made a visitation of that territory.[31]

Few public persons in South Carolina history to that time had attempted to do more for blacks at the risk of their own personal well-being than John England. To the citizenry of the 1820s—from the plantation owners to the peninsula merchants—the Catholic religion was hardly accepted. Yet the bishop's bravery, brilliance and oratorical insights transcended much of the early divide. It was not just his conviction but also his personality that attracted the non-Catholics to his admiration.

The new bishop would have an opportunity to attain an admirable degree of success in Charleston with its smaller contingent of Catholics. He would perform with a fine mind of organizational methodology. Bishop England decided that to manage and administer, he would need to create a constitution for the new diocese. This action stabilized the three-state institution by giving authoritative rule and written reference to its functions.

In 1822, Bishop England had started the new St. Finbar's parish just blocks away on Broad Street, to be operated under the new diocesan constitution he had written. Growth began in this small wooden edifice and would spread throughout the three states. The cessation of the vestry control at St. Mary's, also in 1822, galvanized the Catholic faith to move forward, beyond internal conflict. Bishop John England had become the singular authority to all Catholics in the diocese, now mended and united.

St. Mary's had completed construction of a new church built in 1839 after a citywide conflagration of 1838 destroyed the previous structure. It was Bishop John England who oversaw the replacement church. That handsome church exists today in the heightened grace and elegance exhibited in its caring reconstruction. Its architecture exudes in the warmth of faith.

The broad scope of Bishop England's energy and focus includes his significant travels, yet it was upon the streets of Charleston where his reputation grew. In Charleston, the bishop preached twice on Sundays. He quickly became a popular speaker at secular functions, owing to his worldly sensibilities and brilliant delivery.

The interior of St. Mary's Church, Charleston, completed in 1839. *Photo by author.*

By 1822, Bishop England had organized a Charleston Book Society and, later that year, established the *United States Catholic Miscellany*, the first Catholic periodical published in the United States. It continued to be published until 1861, predating the *Southern Literary Messenger* by more than a decade.[32]

The outspoken bishop opposed nullification (Nullification Act of 1832)[33] in a city where it was highly advocated. England became an active member of the Philosophical Society of Charleston, as well as organizing an Anti-Dueling Society.[34]

Bishop England was quite dismayed by an anti-Catholic oration made by then Secretary of State John Quincy Adams on July 4, 1821. It became the catalyst for what historians consider England's most important and famous speech. He made the trip to Washington to rebut Adams, who had been elected as president of the United States in 1824.

As what would be considered a fact-based and bold oration, Bishop John England defended the faith in front of President John Quincy Adams and others who had been previously dissuaded by Adams of the value of Catholic citizenship. This explanation of Catholicism and the benefit to America was delivered in the U.S. House of Representatives,

The United States Capitol in Washington, scene of the timely Bishop John England speech establishing the separation of church and state in 1826. *Photo by author.*

President John Quincy Adams.
Courtesy of Library of Congress.

and it marked the first time that a Catholic bishop was invited to speak in that chamber. The following selections from the *National Catholic Register* properly present this event that set the record straight about the Catholic view of church and state:

> *What is most important to us today is that Bishop England delivered a memorable speech that boldly proclaimed the beliefs of his faith while at the same time stressing its compatibility with republican virtues...The speech he delivered in Washington January 8, 1826, partly responded to anti-Catholic remarks made by John Quincy Adams in a Fourth of July oration nearly five years earlier. Adams was on hand to hear the bishop's rebuttal...In a preface to the published version of his speech, England said he had sought to address the misunderstanding that even educated people had about the beliefs of the Catholic Church. At several points in the sermon, he discussed the myths that were conveyed regarding Catholic practices, and he most certainly believed Adams was one of those mythmakers. In an age where republicanism—a commitment to equality and virtue—was strongly followed, Bishop England sought to show that Catholicism was perfectly compatible with that ideal. He also endorsed a division between religion and civil government, saying that such a dichotomy was in the best interest of both institutions. One of the bishop's biographers, Peter Clarke, has written, "John England was the first theoretician of separation of Church and state and freedom of religion."*[35]

In the considerable biographical works that have inspected the life of John England, one of the thematic attributes emerges relating him as being a "great apologist." England was well aware of the interpretations—and misinterpretations—of the Catholic religion in the centuries leading up to the Reformation and since.

> *In dissecting this notable speech, the reader is impressed by the steady, but forceful apologia offered by the Irishman. He tells the assembly, which surely was overwhelmingly non-Catholic, that the revelation of truth from the Lord was given to early Church leaders. In the first century these holy men "formed but one Church through many nations—one tribunal to testify in every place the same doctrine—all the individuals who taught, were witnesses for or against each other: the whole body, with the successor of Peter at its head, watchful to see that each taught that which was originally delivered," he said.*

THE

SUBSTANCE OF A DISCOURSE

PREACHED IN THE HALL OF THE

HOUSE OF REPRESENTATIVES OF THE CONGRESS OF THE UNITED STATES,

IN THE

CITY OF WASHINGTON,

ON

SUNDAY, JANUARY 8, 1826.

BY THE RIGHT REV. JOHN ENGLAND, D.D.

BISHOP OF CHARLESTON.

Baltimore:
PUBLISHED BY F. LUCAS, JUN'R.
No. 138 *Market street.*
1826.

The cover of Bishop John England's published address to a joint session of Congress on January 8, 1826.

There has been a constancy to this truth throughout the ages, and it must be presented to each age "neither adding, omitting, [nor] changing." After arguing the static universality of revealed truth, Bishop England then addresses the political issues that were of interest to his republican audience.[36]

In the two-hour sermon, the bishop broached the central subject of John Quincy Adams's earlier argument. There was much to consider in the choice of his delivery and verse as Adams stood in the room for the speech's entirety.

First he discusses the same question that dogged Alfred Smith in his 1928 presidential campaign and John F. Kennedy in 1960: Does a Catholic have inappropriate loyalty to a foreign power—that is, the Pope? Here is where Bishop England is most emphatic.

"I would not allow," he says, "to the Pope or to any bishop of our Church, outside this Union, the smallest interference with the humblest vote at our most insignificant balloting box. He has no right to interference." He then goes a step further by emphasizing that Congress and the U.S. government have no right to meddle in the affairs of the Church. He told the gathering, "You have no power to interfere with my religious rights, the tribunal of the Church has no power to interfere with my civil rights. It is a duty which every good man ought to discharge for his own, and for the public benefit, to resist any encroachment upon either." Unfortunately, he notes, there are misinformed people who believe certain slanders against the Catholic Church. One is that the Church is despotic and antithetical to a republican form of government. He counters by citing Catholic individuals and nations who have been bulwarks against despotism, and argues that there is no evidence that Catholics are anything but true republican patriots.

To the charge that the Church has encouraged persecution, he says that, sadly, every Church has practiced some degree of cruelty and bigotry. This was wrong, but there is nothing in Catholic teaching which encourages it. Even the Inquisition, he notes, was a civil, not a religious, movement.[37]

In the most humble, sincere and succinct tones, the eloquent bishop had diffused nearly every indictment against the coexistence of the Catholic Church and the rights of a democracy. He went on to clarify the role of

Catholics in other governments relating the fear of overthrowing kings. Past European revolutions had been attributed to papal interference.

> *The final political point he addressed dealt with the Church's role in deposing unfriendly kings—clearly a practice that would raise concerns. The evidence, he argues, is absent; and legends to the contrary are the product of biased writers. "It is not," he stresses, "a tenet of the Church that popes interfere with legitimate governments, whether kingdoms or republics."*[38]

After his speech, there were many in Congress impressed enough that they asked for a copy of his notes. The entire speech was later published and given to all in attendance. For Catholics, he had established the separation of allegiance for religious and secular matters. In a matter of weeks, England took an oath to become an American citizen. His commitment to America was formalized. He said, "An American citizen by choice and from adoption, I feel it to be my duty to contribute my humble efforts to sustain the character of our country."[39] Bishop John England was unafraid of defending the Catholic faith in America, as his depth of courage to do so had been well tested in his native Ireland. His profound convictions stood true.

In 1829, Bishop England instituted the Sisters of Charity of Our Lady of Mercy, whose good works included education, a school for girls and the establishment and administration of an orphanage and ancillary centers to assist the less fortunate. Their motherhouse remains in Charleston nearly two centuries later. Bishop England also summoned another order, the Ursulines from Ireland, for additional teaching responsibilities. He established the Philosophical and Classical Seminary of Charleston in 1832 to build the religion upon a seminary. Bishop England also taught at the seminary.[40]

His care for the oppressed gave more insight to his purposeful leadership of the southern church. He was attentive to the plight of the blacks, not only in the city of Charleston but also in the three-state diocese.

He was sent by the Vatican to Haiti in 1834 to seek an accord between that country and the Papacy. That accord, a concordat, was eventually signed by his successor legate, Bishop Joseph Roseti of St. Louis.[41] In all, England made two very difficult trips to Haiti, the last trip testing his health to a point of near death. When travel was, by its nature, arduous and subject to peril, Bishop England persisted with purpose.

St. Peter's Basilica at the Vatican. *Courtesy of Ed Brambley.*

In the interests of his impoverished diocese he visited the chief towns and cities of the Union, crossed the ocean four times, sought aid from the Holy Father, the Propaganda,[42] the Leopoldine Society of Vienna, and made appeals in Ireland, England, France, Italy, wherever he could obtain money, vestments, or books. After Easter, in 1841, he visited Europe for the last time. On the long and boisterous return voyage there was much sickness, and he became seriously ill through his constant attendance on others. Though very weak, notwithstanding, on his arrival in Philadelphia, he preached seventeen nights consecutively, also four nights in Baltimore. With his health broken and his strength almost exhausted, he promptly resumed his duties on his return to Charleston, where he died, sincerely mourned by men of every creed and every party. His apostolic zeal, saintly life, exalted character, profound learning, and matchless eloquence made him a model for Catholics and an ornament of his order.[43]

At five o'clock on the morning of April 11, 1842, Bishop John England died. Platitudes came in from every quarter, well outside Charleston. His life had made a difference, and his death would surely create an un-fillable void. Bishop Francis P. Kenrick of Philadelphia arrived to officiate the funeral Mass before throngs that had gathered well outside the doors of St. Finbar's.

The testimony of the writers and the words of the subsequent eulogy extolled the magnificence of the great and humble man. They expressed the wide reference of his impact to other areas of life beyond his primary spiritual quest.

> *But if we were filled with sorrow, if the unhidden tear flowed at the recollection of the name, the services and virtues of this prelate, let them honor that memory by adhering to the faith, by frequenting the sacraments, by cultivating that universal charity with persons of all climes, denominations and conditions, which it was the great object of his life to see consummated; that his name was dear to humanity; that it was cherished by the philanthropist; that philosophy honored him; that patriotism cherished him—he appealed to them to bear witness. But it was his more meek and fitting province to exhibit him as connected with religion.*[44]

> *Most of his writings were given to the public through the columns of the* United States Catholic Miscellany, *in the publication of which he was aided by his sister, a woman of many-sided ability and talents. His successor, Bishop Ignatius Reynolds, collected his various writings, which were published in five volumes at Baltimore, in 1849.*[45]

Joanna England predeceased her brother, dying in 1827 during a cholera epidemic. She had served him as a secretary, administrator and editor of the *Catholic Miscellany*. Much lamented by brother John, she was buried at St. Finbar's graveyard. Her brother was buried next to her in 1842. Upon the bishop's later exhumation, it was discovered that Joanna's casket had melded to that of her holy brother. It is presumed that the Great Charleston Fire of 1861 that destroyed the newly built cathedral (completed in 1854) melded the two copper caskets together. For this reason, the basement mausoleum that holds the remains of Bishop John England also holds the remains of his sister, Joanna. Joanna England is believed to be among the first females, if not the first, whose remains are contained in a cathedral in the United States.

Bishop England's death was a sad event in 1842 Charleston. He was accorded reverence across the community, notably from non-Catholic admirers. "When Bishop John England, the author of Provincial Councils and the light of the American Hierarchy, died in Charleston on April 11, 1842, all the city's church bells tolled and all flags were set at half-mast."[46]

The vaulted remains of Bishop John England (1786–1842) in the crypt of the Cathedral of St. John the Baptist, Charleston. *Photo by author.*

Bishop England's writing skills were a constant throughout his life. In recognition of his many journalistic efforts, the Catholic Press Association presents an annual publisher's award in his name.[47] His oratory skills were heard well beyond the Holy City, as well.

England inspired others. He changed Charleston. He strengthened a three-state diocese in the South, where Catholicism was a missionary undertaking. He also laid foundations of insight and communication concerning Catholicism that permanently altered the church's standing in America to one of great respect.

Chapter 5

O'BRIEN'S ENGLAND

"THE APOSTLE TO DEMOCRACY"

The refreshing and substantive account rendered by Monsignor Joseph Laurence O'Brien in his extensive 1934 publication titled *John England, Bishop of Charleston: Apostle to Democracy* studies the major aspects of England's twenty-one-year episcopate.

The work of Father O'Brien went well beyond the research and publication of this work. Indeed, it may be surmised that there was not a latter-day biographer outside of Catholic University's Dr. Peter Guilday who studied more about the famous first Charleston bishop. Father O'Brien's contributions to the Diocese of Charleston are quite considerable and will be explored in the subsequent chapters of this work. For now, we will focus on the insightful historic assessment of the brilliance of Bishop John England through the late Monsignor Joseph L. O'Brien, another priest of high eloquence.

O'Brien deftly cites the early bishop's strengths and successes. He uses much of what was available to him in his research, including a personal diary Bishop England began in 1821, the week after his Charleston arrival. Topics included England's patriotic exuberance for his adopted America; his journalistic endeavors, including *The United States Catholic Miscellany*; his personal letters; his determined defense of the Catholic faith; and his role as a teacher. He further explores the role Bishop England played in following the tenets of democracy in the institution of the Catholic Church in America:

Bishop England's strong defense of the Catholic faith brought a talented intellectual to the forefront of the Diocese of Charleston. *Photo from the Palais des Papes, Avignon, by the author.*

> *It is clear that for responsible dissent, for a Catholic Constitution, for democratic Catholic Conventions, for National Councils of the Catholic Church—in short, for the employment of participatory decision-making, of democracy as it flows from the American civil experience in the life of the Catholic Church—Bishop John England of Charleston, South Carolina, provides a premier precedent.*[48]

O'Brien also cites England's resolve in the defense of the Catholic faith as a major credit to his timely leadership. He took it upon himself to graciously answer every challenger.

One long-running letter campaign was a display of John England's intellect. The repartee was reprinted in an 1849 edited collection of letters by Bishop Ignatius Reynolds of Charleston. The point-counterpoint exchange began in July 1839 when a former Episcopal priest turned Baptist minister, Richard Fuller, defended the planned placement of anti-Catholic script on a proposed monument.

Fuller was a gifted orator and had been championed as one of the fine debaters of his day. First in his class at Harvard, Fuller became a Beaufort lawyer before devoting his life to religion. His staunch support of slavery by debate and letters was instrumental in the divide of the American Baptist Church into Southern and Northern Baptist Conventions.[49] His argument against Catholics stirred the public sentiment, inciting response—which Bishop John England so adequately fulfilled.

England was deeply devoted to defending the Catholic faith, as he felt there had been many misgivings and erroneous arguments assaulting it for too long. The exchanges between the two scholars were diatribes researched and positioned as nearly endless rebuttals. These assertions and responses were each reprinted in the *Charleston Courier* as the public became enamored with the excellent high-level debate.

Nearly as remarkable as the zeal in their discourse is the genuine esteem these two religious men had cited for each other in the exchange. The polite dialogue initiated each letter, the salutation being equally complimentary. In the end, Reverend Fuller and Bishop England became friends—mostly built upon mutual respect.

The defense of the separation of church and state, which England had supported in his speech before the U.S. House of Representatives in January 1826, did much to elevate England as the most respected episcopate of his time. Monsignor O'Brien's careful treatment and preservation of the Bishop John England legacy, written twenty years after O'Brien's arrival in Charleston, had other impact than to render a biographical work. O'Brien's publication was distributed as a fine biography and a meticulously researched source material. The key argument for the separation of church and state had been made by England. It would be used one hundred years later to develop political careers for two boys who attended parochial schools in Charleston. Indeed, a student of St. Patrick School, James Francis "Jimmy" Byrnes, would become governor of South Carolina, U.S. secretary of state and U.S. secretary of war (during World War II). Another St. Patrick School student, John P. Grace, would become the first Catholic mayor of Charleston. Monsignor O'Brien, a friend and mentor to the mayor, performed the mayor's eulogy at the Cathedral of St. John the Baptist in June of 1940.

O'Brien explores Bishop England's foray into higher education. Having studied law at Carlow, followed by theology, England was a well-educated prelate. He was most willing to share his knowledge with

St. Patrick's Church, Charleston, where Father Joseph Laurence O'Brien served as pastor from 1929 to 1952. *Courtesy of O'Brien family archives.*

Catholics and non-Catholics alike. O'Brien takes the reader through England's educational background to introduce his intention of building the faith through proper education. He did this through the founding of several educational institutions to include the School for Free Blacks, the Philosophical Society and the seminary. He taught at every opportunity at places well outside the Cathedral pulpit.

O'Brien also researched the private letters and daily journal of the bishop. Bishop England often wrote to his family in Ireland. He wrote to

Rome and Washington. He continually promoted his idea for a bishop's conference through the archdiocese of Baltimore. He wrote personal appeals for funding and requested support clergy. He asked sisters to assist in schools, hospitals and orphanages, founding an order, the Sisters of Charity of Our Lady of Mercy, in 1829.

The founding of *The United States Catholic Miscellany* gave America the first such periodical and established an informative messenger of the Catholic faith that reached well beyond homiletic expression. With the help of England's sister, Joanna, this newspaper helped define the early years of Catholicity in the United States.

In the choosing of Bishop England as the high school name, Monsignor O'Brien provided a reminder of one of America's most important early Catholic personalities. He presented a genuine and heroic patron of the Catholic Church who had dedicated his life to the advancement of Christian values, secular freedoms and public discourse.

Beyond O'Brien's volume, several other biographical depictions of Bishop John England were published, including the edited collection of letters of Bishop England by his successor, Bishop Ignatius Reynolds (1849). *The Works of the Right Reverend John England, First Bishop of Charleston* and other edited volumes by Sebastian G. Messmer, archbishop of Milwaukee, were published in seven volumes (1908). *The Life and Times of John England 1786–1842*, by Dr. Peter Guilday, is in two volumes and serves as a testament of Bishop John England's two-continent endeavors, before and after his arrival in America. It was published in 1927. The fascination with the subject of John England remains.

Chapter 6

CONVICTIONS AND GOVERNANCE

The extraordinary width of John England's life has to be considered within his times, though his intellect and conviction transcended his era. England made four Atlantic crossings when navigation was upon the heavens and the wind and currents, though somewhat predictable, were yet inexact. He also traveled to Haiti twice and to Rome and other European countries. The large masted ships were not as comfortable as ocean liners are today. Sleeping quarters were cramped, and foods were not available as fresh or well preserved. England traveled inland, mostly by horse-drawn carriage, on roads that were dirt corridors subject to the vagaries of weather. He stayed with families, mostly, as there were not hotels in many of the small communities.

Given these conditions, it becomes more astonishing to subtract the travel time away from his life's accomplishments. He would not have been able to write letters during land transit or deliver letters during ocean transit. Yet he was a man of voluminous correspondence, diary entries and regularly published material. He wrote, delivered and preserved his speeches. Until the age of electricity several decades after his time, it was very difficult to produce such works in the evening hours. Yet it could be concluded that John England was a man of letters.

What has written about Bishop John England over nearly two centuries edifies the fascination of this holy man who worked tirelessly within his convictions. England wrote and spoke consistently on these convictions. Yet he is measured beyond his time by a few biographers to some detriment because of this consistency. For instance, England believed that democracy in America was a shining example to the world and some of its tenets would best be applied to the process that the Papacy utilized in the appointment of new bishops:

> *The Sees of Boston and New York are now vacant, or if Prelates have been appointed for them, I am not aware of who they are. They will both be filled before I shall probably address you upon the necessity of having some permanent and known mode of having our Sees filled, not by faction, intrigue or accident—but in a manner more likely to be useful and satisfactory than that which is now in operation.*[50]

Obviously, this did not endear England to the hierarchy of the Roman Catholic Church, but it did reinforce his organizational mindset of what he considered a much better and more appropriate process.

His call for a council of bishops in the United States to meet regularly was not endorsed by the French-born archbishop Ambrose Marèchal but was indeed an organizational nuance that advanced the church in America. It was not until Archbishop Marèchal's death in 1828 that England was able to convince his successor, Archbishop James Whitfield, of the need for these councils. The conjectural resilience and perhaps jealousy of other bishops followed, as in his times of arduous travel, a council of this magnitude may have been quite unpopular. After several iterations, the idea and form followed, and the first Provincial Council of Bishops met in Baltimore in 1829.[51] England's enthusiasm for these meetings served other purposes, as well.

England also advocated conventions for the clergy and laity as part of his constitution for the Diocese of Charleston. He believed that the Catholic Church was primarily "catholic," far-reaching and for all to benefit. Other bishops did not follow, and some, in fact, wrote to Rome to warn of the practice of diocesan constitutions. Nonetheless, the benefits proved to be consistent with the purpose of building a lasting foundation for the Catholic Church in the American South. The diocesan conventions also served another historical function:

> *Consequently his 26 Convention Addresses give a history of the Catholic Church in America for those years. Most importantly, it was through the Convention that the scattered Catholic churches began to grow together with a sense of unity and belonging to a larger church, a*

The statue of Bishop John England at his namesake high school in Charleston (Daniel Island). *Photo by author.*

"catholic" Church, which was their Church where they had both rights and responsibilities.[52]

In the inspection of England's perceived need for a constitution, it appears that his attained enthusiasm for the United States Constitution and the Bill of Rights was applied to the concern over vestries. The lay vestries had been a catalyst for his ordination and assignment to Charleston. In England's opinion, what was written as law in America followed as the form of governance. Thus, he wrote and published a constitution for the three-state diocese and submitted it to Rome.

> *But the people desire to have the Constitution printed, so that they may have a standard by which they may be guided. I have learned by experience that the genius of this nation is to have written laws at hand, and to direct all their affairs according to them. If this be done, they are easily governed. If this be refused, a long and irremediable contention will ensue.* [53]

Though respectful of all others, Bishop England had gained a wide reputation for his intellectual oration and outspoken stance on myriad issues. American slavery was taken to task, though he resided in the port that imported more slaves than any other in the United States. Pundits point out that England did not change slavery or become a martyr for the cause of abolition. Yet the evidence of his strong remarks against the prevailing tide in the American South, in a city that became the kindling of the bonfire that was the American Civil War, leaves no doubt of his conviction. In fact, he took noteworthy action. On the issue, it should be considered that he was sent to Charleston with the primary goal of establishing the Catholic Church in the American South. He did that. Along the way, the most volatile issue he encountered was the abolition of slavery. He had arrived from a country that advocated one culture (the British) controlling another (the Irish). He lived the injustice in his native Cork. England never shied from the discussion and his position that slavery would eventually become abolished, as it did not reconcile with the democratic principles of America's founding. He was ultimately correct but historically in the wrong place and era.

Though the good bishop was widely admired inside his faith and on nearly every periphery, he was not averse to controversy. His consistency was based in the democratic principles he admired. His life's work can best be assessed by the impact of his organizational institutions well beyond his fifty-six years.

Chapter 7

THEY CALLED HIM "DOC"

I t is rare that a person arrives in a community and becomes an immediate agent of progress—a guide for a new age. When the tall and slender Joseph Laurence O'Brien arrived in Charleston at the age of twenty-eight, he made an abrupt impact on the life of numerous Charlestonians well beyond the sphere of Catholicity. The youthful and athletic Catholic priest was well equipped for the tasks he had anticipated.

Like Bishop John England, Father O'Brien inventoried the resources and considered what was absent as much as what was available. There were definitive educational needs evident in Charleston— resources he knew well from his time in the burgeoning Catholic population of Scranton, Pennsylvania, the area that propelled his spiritual upbringing. Scranton and the area nearby had the Catholic formula for growth—parochial schools, convents, hospitals and two seminaries (St. Charles Borromeo and St. Vincent). The Irish and German immigration to the area supported an eleven-county Diocese of Scranton, established in 1868.[54]

Father O'Brien's pre-Charleston existence was immersed in Americana and the Catholic life he enjoyed in the small town of Avoca, less than ten miles from Scranton.

Msgr. Joseph L. "Doc" O'Brien was born 30 April 1884 in Avoca, Pa., to Thomas F. O'Brien and Sarah A. Morahan. His mother was born in England. O'Brien had three brothers and two sisters. He attended

The Avoca, Pennsylvania home of Joseph Laurence O'Brien. *Courtesy of O'Brien family archives.*

Mount St. Mary's Seminary in Emmitsburg, Md., and the Albertinum seminary in Fribourg, Switzerland. Advanced degrees include M.A., S.T.D., and L.L.D.[55]

Father O'Brien became a monsignor in 1934.[56] His nickname, "Doc," may have had Avoca roots, though later students suggested that it came from his first honorary doctorate degree. Nonetheless, he was comfortable with the name in deference to the formality of "monsignor."

O'Brien originally was a seminarian for the Diocese of Scranton. Bishop Henry Northrop adopted O'Brien for the Diocese of Charleston in 1910. He was ordained in Fribourg, Switzerland, on December 15, 1912.[57] The selection of Charleston suited young Father O'Brien, who had long admired and studied the first bishop of Charleston, John England. In many ways, Bishop England was a guide to the young priest's pastoral aspirations.

O'Brien served at Cathedral of St. John the Baptist in Charleston from 1914 to 1929. He was co-founder (with Father James J. May) of Bishop England High School and served as its rector from its beginning in 1915 until 1947. O'Brien became pastor to St. Patrick Parish in Charleston in 1929.[58]

The young priest was a busy man. He traveled to Avoca nearly every summer to visit his family but made the experience productive by teaching literature courses at Marywood College Summer School. He also taught religion and literature courses at the convent of the Sisters of Saints Cyril and Methodius in Danville, Pennsylvania.[59]

His eloquent delivery from the pulpit attracted non-parishioners and friends from across the Charleston community. He was a much-admired banquet speaker, as well as a weekly media personality on WCSC radio, a fine venue for his resonant voice.

His talent for organization and operational strategies became most apparent in his challenging mission of beginning a new high school. But the high school was but one of his brick-and-mortar projects. He was also responsible for the construction of a brick parochial school building on St. Philip Street for St. Patrick's Parish and, later, the renovation of St. Patrick's church and rectory. The original red brick church had been built in 1879.[60] The formation of the high school in 1915 was the first step in a process. The modern planned and engineered high school was built on Calhoun Street in 1921, completed in time for enrollment in the fall

Father O'Brien spearheaded the construction of Wood Memorial School, known as St. Patrick's School, in 1930. *Courtesy of O'Brien family archives.*

of 1922. The replacement high school at Daniel Island was completed seventy-six years later.

It should be noted that Father O'Brien's construction projects took place at times considered inopportune—during World War I and into the years of the Great Depression. Though Father O'Brien arrived in Charleston nearly a century after Bishop John England, he performed these tasks as if he were extending Bishop England's vision for Charleston. The newly arrived priest had become a major catalyst for advancing Catholic education to the high school level, as he had known its impact on Scranton.

O'Brien's emulation of the famous first bishop, John England, became evident in literature. He wrote a biography of the man he felt changed America as the most important episcopate of his time: *John England, Bishop of Charleston: The Apostle to Democracy*. It was published in 1934.

The first bishop and the inventive priest had much in common. Like Bishop England, O'Brien was a fearless innovator. A tall man of formidable presence, he brought a sense of apostolic community from his parochial experiences in Pennsylvania. In Charleston, the primary schools existed ostensibly by the work of the Sisters of Charity of Our Lady of Mercy whom Bishop John England introduced to the diocese. Just as England introduced four sisters in support of primary schools and an orphanage, Father O'Brien recommended additional outside support of religious orders. The high school would need several priests and sisters to teach. By moving Catholic learning to the next level, he also encroached upon the nuance of a coeducational environment. This concept at the high school level had previously been a non-starter, even in public schools, in post-Reconstruction Charleston. The societal precepts of the Victorian age (1837–1901) had cast their shadow on this innovation.

The lower schools existed in 1914 at Cathedral, St. Patrick's and St. Joseph Parishes, and the latter two maintained coeducational status. The Academy of Our Lady of Mercy provided elementary and secondary education for girls only.[61] The academy was administered in the building still in use as the Neighborhood House on North Hampstead Square in Charleston. It was the design of noted Charleston architect Albert Wheeler Todd.[62]

There was little doubt that the high school should be named to honor O'Brien's personal religious model, Bishop John England. The permanent naming of the high school occurred in the second academic year, 1916–17.

The first location of the new high school was simply attached to the See of the Diocese, the Cathedral of St. John the Baptist. The new high school was designated as Cathedral High School. It convened in the auxiliary cathedral school building once used as the church while funds were being raised to rebuild the previous edifice. That first-year effort placed sixty-seven students in four grades: the seventh, ninth, tenth and eleventh.[63] The absence of eighth grade students is not explained, though an eighth grade appeared the following year. It was not until 1948 that the high school added the twelfth grade. Owing to this nuance, there was no graduating class in 1947. In the interim, the seventh and eighth grades were remaindered to the parochial elementary schools.

The diocese did not have to contemplate long for an appropriate naming of the new Catholic high school. The introduction of Father O'Brien's highest recommendation, Bishop John England Memorial High School, was forwarded to Bishop Russell in 1916. Time and convenience unofficially redacted the naming elements of "John" and "Memorial" to simply "Bishop England High School."[64]

In Monsignor O'Brien's own words from his work entitled "John England: A Man of God," he narrates the reason for the naming of the high school after the first bishop:

When the Bishop England High School was in the dangerous days of its infancy, the writer (Monsignor O'Brien) was walking on the Battery with one deeply concerned with the affairs for the Church in South Carolina. Quite unexpectedly, he said to me: "Father, tell me something if you don't mind. Why did you name the high school the Bishop England High School?" I'll summarize my answer.

John England was the first writer or speaker to make the Catholic religion respectable in the estimation of the American public. He restored classical learning in South Carolina. He established the first Catholic weekly journal in the United States. He edited an edition of the Missal for use among his people and revised the catechism in a manner suitable to their needs. He founded the Sisters of Our Lady of Mercy. He was, in his lifetime, the greatest apologist and is yet the greatest apologist the United States has known. He was a preacher of such magnetism that Protestant churches vied with one another to grant him the use of their pulpits.

He taught us how to appreciate the Protestant position and charted for us the workings of the anti-Catholic mind. He taught us how to organize Catholic Action.

The rectory of St. Patrick's Church, Charleston, circa 1947. Father O'Brien resided at this location from 1929 until his death in 1952. *Courtesy of May Forest Archives.*

When he was chosen bishop, he was considered by the Congregation of the Propagation of the Faith the most courageous, the most zealous, the most eloquent of his contemporaries. As a bishop, up to the hour of his death, he was the most courageous, the most zealous, the most eloquent member of the American Hierarchy. And to this day, I am convinced that he still remains the most courageous, the most zealous, the most eloquent bishop the United States has known. I hope the school will become the monument worthy of his genius.[65]

The quest to advance Catholic education and to supply the region with well-trained students within the discipline of the Catholic faith became the focus of Father O'Brien. He was determined to recruit assistance from others for the benefit of all.

In a request to Mrs. Ida Ryan in New York, Father O'Brien mentioned the second-year enrollment of 82 "with room to grow to 150 students." Father O'Brien asked for other support to grow the school, settling on a need of $2,000. Mrs. Ryan had previously donated the former home of the Cenacle Sisters near Calhoun and Pitt Streets for the interim use of the high school.

Unfortunately, Mrs. Ryan declined in a terse response letter dated April 19, 1917:

Rev. dear Fr. O'Brien,
Am sorry but have on hand all I can undertake.
Yours sincerely,
Ida M. Ryan,
Suffern, NY.

The letter to Mrs. Ryan mentioned the faculty: five sisters at twenty dollars per month each and three teaching priests who were unpaid. Importantly, O'Brien noted his dream for the school—that it become an endowed institution.

On March 17, 1916, Father O'Brien presented one of the great American orators of his day, Bourke Cockran, to address the Catholics of Charleston about the importance of a Catholic education. Cockran, after some juxtaposing of schedule, became the Hibernian Society banquet speaker for the evening, with festivities of St. Patrick's Day surrounding the event. Tickets were sold for fifty cents, reserved seats for seventy-five cents. The Hibernian Society postponed its annual banquet dinner until 9:30 that evening to give its membership the opportunity to hear Bourke Cockran.[66]

Retired Confederate colonel James Armstrong, who was himself described by Confederate general Robert E. Lee as "the bravest man he ever knew," introduced Congressman Cockran. Armstrong was serving as the president of the Hibernian Society. Cockran's lecture title, listed in the O'Brien family archival documents, was "St. Patrick, the Effect of His Mission on the Revival of Letters."[67]

Cockran, born in Ireland's County Sligo,

New York congressman Bourke Cockran made the appeal for Catholic education at the high school level in Charleston during his 1916 visit. *Courtesy of National Archives.*

had become an American citizen and was voted to five non-consecutive terms in the U.S. Congress. He was said to have once dated Winston Churchill's mother and, later, mentored young Winston on the art of public speaking. Cockran was also considered largely responsible for the close election of President William McKinley in 1896.[68] As one considered among the finest orators of his day, he gave Father O'Brien and the Diocese of Charleston much-needed momentum in their quest to build a new high school.

In other notes, Father O'Brien gives much credit to the Cockran speech of 1916 as the major persuasion to the Catholics of Charleston for the importance of a Catholic high school. But the collection plate had to be passed outside the church aisles. Indeed, money had to be raised, a curriculum chosen, discipline established and a faculty assembled. The second year of the high school brought new challenges.

In a letter circulated in 1916 to the parents of the students, O'Brien wrote, "For the first time in the history of Charleston, an open air Mass will be celebrated." Father O'Brien built the momentum.

Bishop William T. Russell presided at the closing ceremonies on the school grounds for the first year at Calhoun Street, on June 17, 1917, at 5:30 p.m. Bishop Russell was most supportive of the new high school.

The archival correspondence of Monsignor O'Brien gives compelling testimony to his educational and vocational insights. Twenty-two Catholic men signed a pledge to raise funds as necessary for the support of the first year on Calhoun Street (the second year of the high school). They sought two hundred subscribers at $10 each to defray the expected annual cost of operating the school—only $2,000. The initial group of students included fifty-four boys and thirteen girls. There were eighty-one total enrolled in the second year.

It is noteworthy that in the face of his proposition that the high school be coeducational, Father O'Brien took another great risk. Catholics, and others, were loath to have their daughters attend the same school as boys, with profound concern for proper oversight. Father O'Brien assured parents that he would assume the direct responsibility. There were no contemporary coeducational high schools in Charleston. However, Catholic boys and girls had attended coeducational parish elementary schools since 1906.

Father O'Brien thought it important to impose the guidelines of restraint, as he felt necessary. On January 10, 1917, he issued a circular to the parents of the coeducational high school students. The circular was also published in the *Charleston News and Courier*. It advised parents against the two social concerns of the day: movies and dancing. Movies were in their infancy as black-and-white action films without voices, interrupted by the post of a placard reciting what was to be said or thought. "Talkies" were not in theaters until a full decade later.[69]

In dancing, the tango had already arrived, but the new craze was dancing to jazz.[70] Father O'Brien warned the parents:

> *The age is amusement mad, and not mad on healthy amusement; and a boy or a girl who is going to resist this spirit must have an excellently formed character…To come to the point, there are two great dangers which confront your sons and your daughters—two great dangers which have already undermined the moral nature of many boys and girls, and your boy and your girl may be the next. And both you and I will fail in our duty unless we shield them by word and example. What are these dangers? DANCING for boys and girls who are at the formative ages, and MOVING PICTURES, which are poisoning their imagination and visualizing refined sin before their eyes. Already I hear objections… but if you and I hope to win out we must smash down these objections.*[71]

He was way ahead of his time in his daily observations. The century beyond plunged impressionable children into many more "mad amusements." Surely he would have written about edgy satirical cartoons, violent action movies and the preponderance of social media, among other cultural "advances."

The entire faculty was composed of Monsignor O'Brien; his assistant, Father James J. May (for whom the present-day May Forest Motherhouse on James Island is named); and four sisters of the Sisters of Charity of Our Lady of Mercy, founded by Bishop England.[72]

In 1921, while the original building on Calhoun Street was being razed, BEHS rented space at Gregorian Hall on George Street.

The cornerstone of the new main building in 1921 commemorated the hierarchal authorities listed in the O'Brien notes: "Pope Benedict XV, President Warren G. Harding, Governor R.A. Cooper, Mayor John P. Grace" and then-bishop of Charleston William T. Russell.[73] The new high school was dedicated to "Saint Paul, the Apostle of the Gentiles."[74]

Father O'Brien embarked upon a major fundraising campaign. For this, he needed wide diocesan support and an expert fundraising accomplice. The Catholic population in Charleston remained small, yet it

Father James J. May, a native of Charleston, was an expert fundraiser. *Courtesy of May Forest Archives*.

was imperative that substantial funds were raised among this community for the establishment of the new high school in its permanent site of 1922. For that task, Father O'Brien recruited the very capable Father

James J. May. Father May was another outstanding communicator, but more importantly, he was a taskmaster. Together, Fathers O'Brien and May began a plan that would become a modern high school that would reach into Charleston's future.

While Father O'Brien carefully detailed his timing and strategy in raising the $50,000 needed to build the new high school and also to furnish the rooms with desks, chairs and teaching aids within the grand total, he needed key assistance. Father James J. May (1887–1958) was charged with the responsibility of organizing the fundraising for the new high school. May, who had been ordained in 1913, later served St. Francis Xavier Infirmary as the lead fundraiser for its addition in 1926. He became the director of Catholic charities for the diocese and the director of Catholic cemeteries. He served as rector of the Cathedral Parish from 1928 to 1950. Much beloved, he made many selfless contributions to the Charleston community and beyond. May assisted Monsignor O'Brien with renovations to St. Patrick's Church and helped raise funds for the Wood Memorial School. He also performed admirably in support of American troops during both World War I and World War II. Notably, he led the fundraising effort for the new convent for the Sisters of Charity of Our Lady of Mercy, a beautiful site that bears his name, May Forest, on James Island. Elevated to monsignor in 1934, May was selected as vicar general of the Diocese of Charleston.[75]

Father May showed a skillful exuberance for the task of encouraging the funding for the new high school. He devised a plan to inspire teams of Catholics from across the city. He incorporated two competing teams: thirteen teams of ladies and ten teams of men. Typically, each team had seven members. Prominent early twentieth-century Charleston names emerged from these lists: Molony, Croghan, Schachte, McCarthy, Hartnett, O'Neill, Budds, LeTellier, Trouche, Devereux, Lighthart, Duffy, Grace, Erickson, Matson, Furlong, McAlister, Moran, Comar, Rooney, Dengate, Storen, Igoe, Beshere, Albenesius, Maguire, Hollings, Jarvis, Murphy, Gibson and Lowry. One could recognize these early names evolving as yet more street names, buildings and prominent businesses a century later. Mrs. J.J. Furlong chaired the women's effort. Mr. M.A. Condon chaired the men's division. Mr. A.W. Litschgi was named as the general chairman for the entire project by Father O'Brien.[76]

Of those early contributors listed, so many others became highly recognized Charleston families many decades later, including Riley, Condon, Magrath, Oliver, Burmester, Leonard, Brandt, Cosgrove,

Father May divided fundraising teams between the men and women of the diocese. Both teams met regularly at Knights of Columbus Hall on Calhoun Street. *Courtesy of BEHS Archives.*

Brennan, Sottile, Cantwell, Souberoux, Michel, Aimar, Bouvette, Hanley, Bicaise, Barbot and Livingston. These Charleston names endured. Some are associated with place names that have emerged from them or their progeny, such as Cosgrove Avenue, Riley Park, Sottile Theater and others.

The fundraising teams met monthly at the new Knights of Columbus Hall on Calhoun Street, whose foyer marble lists a building committee from 1908 that reveals many of the same names. Meetings would include remarks from speakers who reminded the fundraisers of why they were building a high school that taught religion. One speech by a businessman spoke to the need of properly trained women to type and take shorthand notes, pointing out that the Charleston businesses would hire them upon completion of their coursework.

The Reverend P.N. Lynch Council 704 hosted these monthly fundraising meetings, usually with a meal and a speaker, at the expansive Knights of Columbus Hall, without charge. One monthly speaker, Reverend Father Hyland, reminded the assemblage in June 1919, "You are preparing the greatest defense of our nation."[77] He warned with a tale about a country without higher education that would fall prey to those that were educated. His speech was a post–World War I message that warned of future wars.

The final fundraising reports summed $84,118—well more than the initial $50,000 goal that had since been adjusted up to $75,000. The reports showed that the ladies obtained more donors and the men more funds. There were significant funds raised among non-Catholics, again by some foundation names of the community: Pringle, Marjenhoff, Solomon, McDowell, Patrick, Faber, Cotton, Young, Blalock and Van Smith.[78]

Upon completion of construction for the new school, Bishop Russell officiated at the opening ceremony. Bishop Russell's comments that day extolled the work of Father O'Brien and the Catholics of Charleston:

"Our High School is completed. It was built by the hard-earned money of the Catholics of this Diocese. It is out of debt," Bishop Russell began.

"When the passerby asks what building this is in the heart of Charleston, surrounded by its spacious grounds, and is told that it is a Catholic high school, he will conclude that the Catholics of Charleston appreciate higher education. It will be evident that those who planned, worked for, and completed this undertaking are determined that their children shall have an opportunity to make themselves something more than hewers of wood and drawers of water.

"Facts are stubborn things. This institution is a fact. We have dreamed of it, and sometimes in the past, a high school was in the planning. Today it is a fact. When I first proposed to build a high school for $36,000, I was told it is impossible. With willing hands and loving hearts nothing is impossible. You have placed in my hands not merely the money I asked, but you have completed a high school of sixteen rooms, including an assembly hall capable of accommodating three hundred, at a cost of more than $56,000; and, besides, you have borne the expense of running the old high school for two years. Altogether, since you have put your shoulders to the wheel, you have, besides supporting your three parochial schools and the convent, contributed to education through this high school about $65,000.

"The credit for beginning this high school in Charleston belongs to Father O'Brien. He planned it, he worked for it, he made it such

Bishop England High School as it appeared in 1923. *Courtesy of BEHS Archives.*

a success that you bravely tore down the old building on this site and determined to erect a new high school that would be worthy of its director, the Sisters, the children, and the education that was given in this institution.

"The Catholics of Charleston can never be too grateful to Fr. O'Brien for what he has done for their children."[79]

Father O'Brien set the curriculum. Every student studied Latin. Each student had five classes per week in religion, specifically studying the New Testament. The "commercial" courses were typing, stenography and penmanship. Five classes per week were given in math and English, and another five were split with American history and geography. No class had more than twelve students. By the year's end, eleven students had left for reasons not given.[80]

An interesting note found in the O'Brien family papers from July 5, 1916, gives insight into Father O'Brien's demanding curriculum and those who would and would not meet the requirements: "If an honor roll were published it would contain most of the names of those enrolled. We refrain from publishing the names of those who failed in class work or in conduct, in as much as such publication would serve no good purpose."[81] Father O'Brien preferred the optimism of a positive result.

Founding the high school furthered the education of young people into two distinct course areas: the commercial business field and the classical learning field. As O'Brien progressed within the new assignment, he also participated in assisting others in other communities.

Between 1943 and 1945, Monsignor O'Brien served the state and the country at the National Conference of Christians and Jews.[82]

These conferences were performed at U.S. military camps and U.S. Army air bases with the charge to forge better understandings among those fighting for freedoms and the American way of life.

As radio became a popular mode of communication, Monsignor O'Brien worked with a local station, WCSC, to host a Sunday program. By testimony from his contemporaries, it was a show not to be missed. His resonant voice, according to one former student and program listener, was both forceful and full of encouragement.

Father O'Brien also served the Diocese of Charleston as the superintendent of Catholic schools. This effort produced measurable growth in parochial school building throughout the state, bringing the benefit of parochial education to the growing cities of Columbia and Greenville.

His later years were spent at the rectory of St. Patrick's Church, where he had resided since 1929. There, he was able to write daily letters to former students, friends and family. He died there on the morning of March 2, 1952, at the age of sixty-seven. The Mass of Christian burial

The funeral of Monsignor Joseph L. "Doc" O'Brien on March 6, 1952. *Courtesy of O'Brien family archives.*

The monument to Monsignor O'Brien was dedicated in September 1952. It is situated at the front entrance of St. Patrick's Church, Charleston. *Photo by author.*

and subsequent interment were well attended. The size of the crowd forced authorities to close St. Philip Street for the duration of the service. A much-loved holy man had passed from the earth.

Chapter 8

TWO PRIESTS OF CHARLESTON

Through the study of Bishop John England, and with the help of Dr. Peter Guilday's works and that of Monsignor O'Brien within his family papers, some comparisons are imminent.

Bishop England and Monsignor O'Brien each had a sister who became a nun and a brother who became a priest. Bishop England's sister remained in Ireland, though he did have an additional sister, Joanna, who dedicated much of her life to the bishop's assistance. His brother Thomas R. England served a parish at Passage West (Cork) until he died from the Irish famine in 1847. He was cherished for his caring of the prisoners of Spike Island (a jail much like San Francisco's Alcatraz) in Cork Harbor.

Bishop England's sister Mary was a brilliant student and teacher. In 1811, she entered the North Presentation Convent in Cork—the very same convent where her brother John served nearly ten years as chaplain. She took the name Sister Catherine from St. Catherine of Siena. The North Presentation Convent remained her home until her death in 1872, thirty years after her brother's death in Charleston. Bishop England returned to Ireland three times (1832, 1834 and 1841). It was an express command of Cork's Bishop Murphy that disallowed Sister Catherine England to join her brother in Charleston in the year 1834. Sister Catherine led a dedicated life of teaching and tending to the sick. She was versed in Latin, French, Spanish, German and Greek.[83]

Sister Mary Gerald O'Brien, OLM, served the Diocese of Charleston from 1916 to 1984. *Courtesy of O'Brien family archives.*

Father O'Brien's brother William became a priest and served a parish in Brooklyn, New York. Sister Mary Gerald O'Brien entered the Our Lady of Mercy community in 1916 and served the diocese until her death in 1984.[84] Father O'Brien's only other brother, Tommy, followed Father O'Brien to Charleston and assisted him. He eventually married and moved to Columbia, South Carolina. It is from the descendants of the Columbia family of brother Thomas O'Brien that many of the 2014 private family documents and letters have been preserved.

These non-contemporaneous church leaders, England and O'Brien, left significant impressions on their admiring contemporaries and a lasting heritage to their diocese. There were other obvious similarities.

Both Bishop England and Father O'Brien were ordained abroad, with England taking holy orders in Cork, Ireland, and O'Brien receiving his holy orders in Fribourg, Switzerland. Both came to Charleston as part of a missionary status since Catholicism was only about 1 percent of the diocesan population of their era. Both were responsible for recruiting holy women. Bishop England founded the Sisters of Charity of Our Lady of Mercy (1829) and further recruited the Ursuline order. Monsignor O'Brien needed teaching assistance from outside the Diocese of Charleston. Bishop Russell agreed and the Sisters of Saints Cyril and Methodius responded, and later the Oblate Sisters of Providence did as well. Both England and O'Brien served as teachers and professors, each at the college level. Both were authors, the bishop as a constant contributor to periodicals in his native Ireland and, later, as founder of *The United States Catholic Miscellany*. Monsignor O'Brien penned many contributions to journals and wrote his life's work in 1934, *John England, Bishop of Charleston: Apostle to Democracy*. Their homilies and public addresses are much preserved for other ages. Both were non-adversarial personalities, extending sincere courtesies to others outside the Catholic faith. Both exhibited brave leadership within firm principles by their profound convictions. They were both considered academics with a propensity for research and enlightenment. Both were masters of organizational procedures, preferring to recruit people toward a common strategy.

The legacy that was Father O'Brien has breached a century through the trifold mission of spirituality, academic prowess and physical growth for the high school he named. The forging of the brand Catholic in the Diocese of Charleston was a die cast by the Corkman, Bishop John England. Through the efforts of Father O'Brien and Father James J. May, the strength of that educational component metal has held true.

In its natural progression, it should be noted that other selfless priests have also made monumental contributions, each in their own style, to the tremendous benefit of the high school. These include a most devout Reverend John L. Manning (as rector, 1947–59), the tall and resonant orator Reverend William J. Croghan (1959–64), the personable

A dinner to honor Father John L. Manning, 1927. Manning became rector at BEHS in 1947. *Courtesy of BEHS Archives.*

Monsignor Robert J. Kelly (as rector, 1964–90) and the incomparable wit and insight exhibited by Monsignor Lawrence B. McInerny throughout his stint as rector, which began in 1990.

Proudly, Bishop England High School was the first integrated high school in the state of South Carolina and featured the first South Carolina High School League minority athlete in the person of Arthur McFarland. McFarland graduated with honors and furthered his education at the University of Notre Dame and the Law School at the University of Virginia, returning to Charleston to eventually become a municipal judge, among other accomplishments. Other quite notable graduates include the ten-term mayor of Charleston, Joseph P. Riley Jr.; former United States congressman Thomas F. Hartnett; and the entrepreneurial mayor of the burgeoning town of Mount Pleasant, John J. Dodds Jr.

A crucifix at Palais des Papes, Avignon, France, at dusk. *Photo by author.*

There are compelling numbers of more-than-notable graduates from varied fields and professions who have benefited from the broad and enlightened Catholic education afforded at BEHS.

Bishop England High School has earned a wide spiritual, educational and athletic reputation unmatched in South Carolina. The one-hundred-year result is to be both celebrated and appreciated. The alumni, students, parents and faculty should be ever mindful of the sacrifices of its founders, the now eponymous names of John England and Joseph Laurence "Doc" O'Brien, two priests who have built a lasting value enjoyed by many generations.

There are immutable laws of earth that cannot be violated. There is the law of gravity. There is life as well as death. There is time and mass, finite math—and irrefutable science. And there are secular laws that are supported by laws that God put forth. The Apostle Matthew writes of Christ's law in chapter 22, verses 37 to 40, where he reveals: "You shall love the Lord, your God, with all your heart, with all your soul, and with all your mind. This is the greatest and the first commandment. The second is like it: You shall love your neighbor as yourself. The whole law and the prophets depend on these two commandments."

It is the love of Christ and love of their fellow man that is seen as thematic in the lives of both priests. Yet there were struggles. To make a

Father O'Brien brought a new sense of Catholic growth through education to Charleston. *Courtesy of O'Brien family archives.*

mark of success, one must often overcome obstacles of the journey that may seem impassable.

For Bishop John England, adversity was his birthright. It commanded his early environment, wrought with the restrictions of a ruling class. He was further challenged with a large missionary state more than five times the size of his home country. This vast territory became his diocese in what was mostly a wilderness. He faced the bigotry of the Old World in the general societal dislike of Catholicism. Slavery was in effect, with Charleston as the foremost American port of that practice. There was a dearth of funding and resources, so much so that he traveled back to Europe four times to raise funds and recruit personnel assistance in the form of sisters and priests. Travel was a most difficult challenge.

Monsignor O'Brien had similar impairment as a newly ordained priest from Pennsylvania moving to the South where there remained a vestige of Yankee animosity. In short order, he faced a world war, an influenza pandemic, the age of Prohibition and the Great Depression. In all this chaos, he remained vigilant in his purpose to establish the high school. He raised funds—with the help of Father May—when there was very little to be donated. His vision of a Catholic coeducational high school may have been a tough sell during difficult times. He saw young men whom he had taught enter a Second World War and comforted families when some did not return. The deficiencies never dissuaded him from his pastoral duties. He performed as if divine providence had guided him to each stage.

Though the world presented itself to be constant in its eternal strife, whether it had been Penal Codes, extreme bias, two world wars or economic depression, John England and Joseph Laurence O'Brien lived Christ's message. The commonality they enjoyed was the love for all God's diverse children. Their adherence to the principle of "love God, love thy neighbor" can be gleaned from all that is written and spoken about their disconnected lifetimes. The celebratory evaluation of a one-hundred-year-old high school is, ostensibly, a celebration of these two lives.

There are holy waters to behold—refreshed, renewed and re-inspired for the centuries that will follow. They have flowed forth and blessed a mighty flock.

Chapter 9

FOUNDATIONS

John England brought a fledgling America to a sense of meaningful progress well beyond his three-state diocese. He built foundations of organization, democratic principles, scholarship and learning, care for humankind and fundamental separations that are evident two centuries hence. He built essential interreligious trust that scarcely existed before his impact. He established important dialogue and written communication among Catholics, political entities, independent countries, the Vatican and even his own clergy. He fearlessly stated and reinforced his well-based and articulated principles, though they were not always popular.

In building a foundation to a high school, the mental image of bricks and mortar gives way to the iconic image of the mission it would embrace. After all, several state-of-the-art buildings of brick and mortar that were once the new Bishop England High School no longer exist. Yet the foundation mission that Father O'Brien envisioned remains. He wanted to advance Catholic education to a level that heretofore had not existed in the Holy City of Charleston. He did so without wavering. In doing so, he continued the vision of the first prelate, John England. The foundation of developing young people—male and female—in the enrichment of faith, physical endeavor and educational prowess remains. His vision of reaching into local media, particularly the nuance of radio broadcast, had scarcely been done by other priests nationally. His ability to reach others outside the faith was quite mindful of the bishop he had studied before coming to Charleston.

A painting of buildings in Charleston. *By Charlotte Simmons McQueeney.*

Bishop John England avowed his vision of a world enraptured by freedoms even while under duress. It was this foundation of thought that persisted in his position of "vindicating the political rights of his countrymen...but asserting their liberty of conscience."[85] The foundation of freedom is, as Thomas Jefferson described in the American Declaration of Independence, an "inalienable" right. It is unassailable. Though it must be protected all too many times, freedom is a many-faceted diamond of undeniable beauty. The foundation of freedom is the foundation of choice, of speech, of protest and of religion. England saw the democracy that grew from this foundation as the most important institution of the secular society known to his world. He wanted it protected and its benefit to be spread.

Foundations can wash away should they not be anchored deep and wide, should they not be constructed of unfailing material. To the edification of future generations, the foundations set forth by Bishop John England and Monsignor Joseph Laurence O'Brien meet the Builder's specifications. Real foundations are made of trust.

Out of chaos comes order in the comportment of civilization and in the movements of the universe. From the complex, the simple can be deduced. The two priests who have made compelling contributions to the growth of faith in Charleston and beyond had the finely suited mindset of orderliness. True leaders of generations have this gift. They are able to set in motion a pattern of complexity aimed at a result of simplicity through institutions that make that course beneficial to others generations away. They created holy orders, learning centers and charitable traditions that have arrived at our contemporary era. They were as selfless as the person who plants an acorn for future populations to enjoy the swirling beauty of an oak.

Catholicism has flourished in the See of the Diocese, Charleston. Initially, England found the three states with less than 1 percent Catholic population. The Holy City and its metropolitan area have more Catholics than the other large metro areas of the state, now at 8 percent. Other large metropolitan cities in the original diocese have grown as well. Charlotte has 9.7 percent, Savannah 8.5 percent, Atlanta 16 percent and Raleigh 6 percent.[86] The Catholic Church continues to grow in the American South, but that region has been historically the least populated by the papists.

In some instances, foundations are laid in the faith that they will be built upon by others. Completion can be an ongoing commitment that crosses generations. It is interesting to ponder the words of Bishop Francis Kenrick of Philadelphia on the subject of John England being underutilized in his role in Charleston:

> [The] *Charleston diocese is not a fit theatre for a man of his splendid talents…and I would at any moment resign my mitre to make place for him. This I authorize you to communicate to the Sacred Congregation…I had proposed him for the administration of New York, which most sadly needs an efficient Prelate.*[87]

It may have been that England was in the right place after all. The South was in need of strong leadership and found in England a man unafraid of speaking his mind but most willing to show respect for all factions. He laid a foundation in a place where it would not likely have been otherwise laid for many decades. His foundation of trust and service became a model for the bishops who followed and especially for the monsignor Joseph Laurence O'Brien to emulate.

O'Brien, too, left much to be completed above the original stonework. In the following decades, other priests, sisters, laity and volunteers have

IN MEMORY OF G. W. AIMAR

A stained-glass window at St. Mary's Church, built in 1839. The parish dates to 1789. *Photo by author.*

expanded his work to more comprehensive applications for a more demanding world. The enhancement of a broad education inclusive of religious training and insight makes the high school O'Brien founded appropriately placed in time. It has adapted well.

The men who have brought a compelling wave of fervor to places that were previously barren have left a legacy. Their foundation of faith remains through landmark organizations, educational advancements and their subsequent orchestration of each.

Chapter 10

A MAN FOR ALL TIMES

It may be that there can only be one person of an age who defines his time such as John England from the late eighteenth to mid-nineteenth centuries. He administered to his constituency, the Catholic Church and its flock, most graciously. He went beyond to build a lasting legacy that has inspired numerous volumes of great books in the years well past his lifetime. The aspects of the man are as countless color shades upon a prism. And like a prism, the sight of the richness of hue mesmerizes the onlooker with each dancing ray of sunlight. There will be those reading about John England with profound fascination into the coming centuries.

The process of beatification and canonization to sainthood is the distinct course of action reserved to the pontiff. This is a most diligent procedure that inspects the lives of very holy men and women across the Catholic faith. There is but one proper manner by which canonization can be proposed and accomplished. However, there is at least one source of public discourse that suggests the beatification and sainthood of Bishop John England. Authors Leonard Swidler and Ingrid Shafer of the Association for the Rights of Catholics in the Church (ARCC) advocate the inspection of the lives of both Archbishop John Carroll and Bishop John England as potential American saints.[88]

The authors assemble an impressive argument supporting the cause for beatification. In doing so, they inspect Bishop England's contemporary prelates to include those opposed to some of his visionary changes. They

St. Peter's Basilica. The process of sainthood begins with the pope in Rome. *Courtesy of Giorgio Galeotti.*

cite the personal relationship and appreciation he had gained from Pope Gregory XVI. They relate the admiration of others, including President Andrew Jackson and Secretary of State Martin Van Buren. They point to the bishop's two-continent accomplishments, as well as his proposals of changes that occurred after his lifetime—changes he authored with a futuristic disposition.

Notably, he thrived in a diocese that was 99 percent non-Catholic and earned lasting friendships well beyond those who shared his Catholic faith. He advocated national councils for bishops, which were granted in his lifetime and continue today, although they were not immediately embraced. He preached in churches of other denominations to perform the Catholic Mass, thankful for the beneficence of other religious leaders who allowed the use. He preached before the South Carolina state legislature frequently, by invitation. His adherence to austerity and poverty built admiration and trust in a community of considerable affluence. He was not a man of insular stances when others advocated such. He supported democracy as an intrinsic value to be invested both secularly and inside the institutions of faith. His masterful use of language and inflection were indicators of a brilliant mind brilliantly utilized. His death was mourned locally, nationally and internationally.

Angels and saints depicted on the inside of the dome of St. Peter's Basilica, the Vatican. *Photo by author.*

One reference from Father Baker, the chaplain of the Washington Light Infantry at the time of England's passing, eloquently summarizes his impact among his diocese as well as his country and community:

> *That it is with no ordinary feelings of sorrow that the company this publicly recognizes the loss from among its members of the Right Reverend Bishop England. The eloquent tones that have stirred our hearts as with the sound of a trumpet shall no more command and arrest our attention. The lips ever devoted to the advancements of virtue and religion are forever mute, frozen into silence by the icy hand of death. The earnest vindicator of the liberty of his native land, the devoted admirer and constant advocate of the institutions of this, his adopted country; the man of unimpeached and unimpeachable character, of intellect and acquirements wide and far-reaching, of imagination fervid and poetic— the priest of self-denying and self-sacrificing virtues, whom all men of every sect and faith delight to honor—the careful and sleepless watcher over the flock committed to his care—has finished his earthly course.*[89]

Though his life's work and forward vision may continue to be scrutinized and estimated for their significance, there might never come a day when the papacy will elevate this humble man to the level of saintly consideration. It is for those who study and evaluate his life and times today to ascertain a relevance to our own lives. Where would the Catholic Church in America be had John England never arrived at our harbor? Where would the struggles of his native Ireland be without his brave writings? Where would the discourse of interreligious communication and tolerance have diverted? Bishop John England truly changed his times and the times hence.

Chapter 11

THE NAMESAKE HIGH SCHOOL IN

ITS FIRST HUNDRED YEARS

The high school that bears the name of the great bishop and was established by the great monsignor is now at a celebratory age. There are decades of growth nurtured by clergy and laity alike. Indeed, the first lay principal of the high school made a remarkable impact. Nicholas J. Theos operated the high school as a business from 1973 to 1998, its last year on Calhoun Street. Other capable principals, David Held and Michael Bolchoz, have followed. Patrick Finneran leads the high school into its second century.

Father O'Brien had a concise vision for the high school project. Of note were the three short tenets found in the private papers of the O'Brien family tendered to the diocesan archives in 2014. "We want to build a high school whose students will excel academically, physically, and spiritually," he wrote in a letter to Bishop Henry P. Northrop in November 1914.[90]

Timing was right, and the enthusiasm of the Catholic community prevailed. The standing, a full century later, of Bishop England High School reflects encouraging results.

Students' annual SAT scores merit among the highest in the state of South Carolina each and every year. The school's wide academic mission has grown into a college preparation curriculum, with most students extending their education well beyond the twelfth grade. Its website shows that over the current seven-year graduation statistics, the school produced a 98 percent rate of progression of its students into higher

First lay principal Nicholas J. Theos (right) administered the high school for twenty-five years. Father Robert J. Kelly (below) served as rector from 1964 to 1990. *Courtesy of BEHS Archives.*

education. Students from Bishop England High School usually fare very well at higher levels of education. The high school has also boasted multiple generations of students from many local families, in addition

A Century of Catholic Education

The centennial banner (left) adorns the Daniel Island school (below), completed in 1998. *Photos by author.*

The dedication of the Bishop John England statue in front of Bishop England High School in the fall of 1950. *Photo by Albert Sottile. Courtesy of BEHS Archives.*

to the infusion of other like-minded families newer to the Charleston area. It has become a popular private alternative to the public school system, even for non-Catholics. Student population has generally ranged from 650 to 800 students, though the new forty-acre campus on Daniel Island can expand to house as many as 1,100 students. It was built in anticipation of that eventual growth. It remains a popular academic challenge to students who seek a proper foundation for degrees beyond high school.

The physical mission can likely be interpolated into the performance of the school's many athletic teams spanning the past century. Though Doc O'Brien was an avid basketball fan and oversaw the plans for the school's first basketball gymnasium shortly before his 1947 retirement as rector, he could not have imagined the lofty degree of its athletic prowess. Bishop England High School athletic teams have won well in excess of one hundred state championships—touching every sport, male and female—in that time. They have won more state championships than any other South Carolina high school. An article in *Sports Illustrated*, written in 2005, rated Bishop England High School as the preeminent sports high school in the state of South Carolina and among the best in the country.[91] Another 2013 article in *USA Today* placed the Battling Bishops among the top ten national athletic high school programs.[92] Among the storied coaches at the high school are Gerald F. McMahon (boys' basketball), Jack Cantey (football), Patricia Owens (National High School Coach of the Year, girls' tennis) and Amelia Dawley (National High School Coach of the Year, girls' volleyball). Kathy Blackmon also earned National High School Coach of the Year for girls' volleyball, the sport that has merited more state championships for BEHS than any other.

The graduating class of 1919 in the rear yard of the former Cenacle Sisters Convent, which served as the high school from 1916 to 1922. *Courtesy of May Forest Archives.*

A football game in 1950. *Courtesy of BEHS Archives.*

The Christmas program of 1949. *Courtesy of BEHS Archives.*

Next page, top: Mr. Bishop England John Torlay with Miss Bishop England Caroline Ehrhardt, crowned by Father John L. Manning in 1952. *Courtesy of BEHS Archives.*

Next page, bottom: The 1927 boys' basketball team. Father O'Brien served as rector, teacher, coach, athletic director and manager in the early years of the high school. *Courtesy of O'Brien family archives.*

Father James J. May, as part of the BEHS faculty, addresses the parents. *Courtesy of BEHS Archives.*

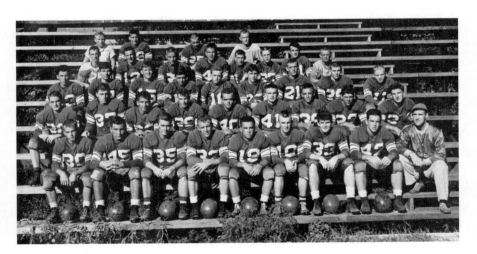

The third year of the football program at BEHS. *Courtesy of BEHS Archives.*

As to the most important mission of spirituality, again there has been heralded success. Not only has the high school graduated many who have dedicated their lives to religious orders and sought other higher religious plateaus in their personal lives, but the aspect of teaching the subject of religion in a focused four-year program has vaulted the school to become the largest non-secular high school in the state. Religion, as many have described, is the major reason that parents send their children to Bishop England High School. Each day is started and ended by prayer, a decided counter to the prevailing secular restrictions imposed on public education.

Cheerleader Barbara Smith chats with basketball player Fred McMahon in 1957. *Courtesy of BEHS Archives.*

The 1927 Lady Bishops (known as the Bishopettes then). *Courtesy of BEHS Archives.*

Homecoming 1951. *Courtesy of BEHS Archives.*

Next page, top: The Bishops built a formidable basketball program in the Father O'Brien Gymnasium. This 1951 game was played against St. Paul's High School. *Courtesy of BEHS Archives.*

Next page, bottom: A student dance in 1971. *Courtesy of BEHS Archives.*

The cover of the 1970 yearbook, *Miscellany*, with art by Agnes White (Zed). *Courtesy of BEHS Archives.*

Students at assembly. *Courtesy of BEHS Archives.*

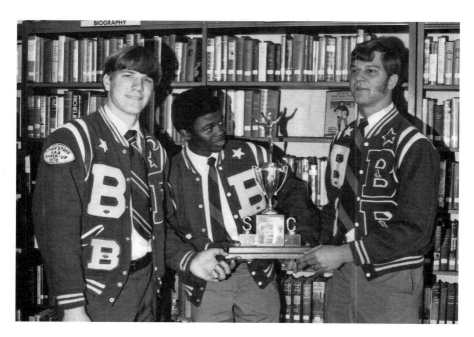

Eddie Westervelt, Keith Jones and Tommy Sakre, all from the class of 1971, hold the conference football championship trophy. *Courtesy of BEHS Archives.*

Opposite, bottom: The parents' assembly in 1949 in the newly constructed Father O'Brien Gymnasium. *Courtesy of BEHS Archives.*

The BEHS Girls' Choir performs a musical, 1956. *Courtesy of BEHS Archives.*

The front of Bishop England High School on Daniel Island. *Photo by author.*

The principal serving the school for the centennial anniversary, Mr. Patrick Finneran, reinforces the visionary aspects of Father O'Brien:

> *The high school is dedicated to the very same principles from that initial year of 1915. We advocate a well-rounded education that includes Father O'Brien's guidelines of educational enlightenment, physical development and spiritual growth. Now, the school appeals to others outside of the Catholic religion. Nearly 25 percent of our students are non-Catholic. But they are equally afforded the same value system we encourage for all. We teach much more than academic lessons here. We even have a program for those with other hardships, and they are able to thrive within the environment we administer with great care. It is an attribute to the founders, the alumni and parents, as well as our current faculty, that Bishop England High School prepares for the new challenges of its second century.*

Ostensibly, Father O'Brien envisioned a need for the development of young people in these three key areas of mind, body and soul. One hundred years later, a century of progress reflects results of which he would be justly proud.

Chapter 12

THE CALL

B uilding a consensus for a need is often an arduous process. In the study of the two Irish-lineage priests who have built foundations of Catholicity and Judeo-Christian brotherhood in Charleston, it became apparent that they thrived at this process. The calling to religious orders has been on decline for several decades. Young gentlemen and young ladies have not been entering religious service in the healthy numbers generated in the past. The calling is both worthy and difficult. Parishes across the United States have either closed or consolidated with others. Catholic hospitals have seen a profound reduction of religious orders dedicated to the sick. Lay teachers have replaced clergy nearly universally. Seminarians are scant; novices are in startlingly regressive numbers. The call is not being heard as it once was.

Perhaps that trend will reverse beyond our lifetimes. There are certainly lives that have been studied, like those of John England and Joseph Laurence O'Brien, that have inspired many others. O'Brien himself was inspired by England. Understanding their impact on the world gives testimony to their respective life's work. They each set standards. Their example alone will be studied well past contemporary times, and others will be stirred to follow. The advent of digital information broadens the scope of their lives long past quills and inkwells.

The beloved priests and sisters have already followed. For instance, a third Irish-lineage priest could be meritoriously added to the specter of greatness ascribed to the modern Bishop England High School.

This 1944 photograph shows the support of the Sisters of Charity of Our Lady of Mercy and Father James J. May as they fed breakfast to troops stationed in Charleston for the duration of World War II. *Courtesy of May Forest Archives.*

Reverend Monsignor Robert J. Kelly (1927–2004), of Hartford, Connecticut, served as rector of Bishop England High School from 1964 to 1990. The young Kelly played professional baseball in the Boston Braves organization from 1945 to 1952. Among his teammate friends was the greatest of the Harlem Globetrotters, Meadowlark Lemon, who played in an inconceivable streak of 9,925 winning basketball games.[93] Lifelong friends, Lemon visited Father Kelly on occasion at the 203 Calhoun Street campus. Personally humble, Father Kelly's sports abilities sealed many friendships in other communities before arriving in Charleston. But it was in Charleston that he was cherished.

Father Kelly was ordained in 1953. His exceptional athletic talent was often demonstrated on the baseball diamond and tennis courts and in the aptly named Father O'Brien Gymnasium, where he played pickup games with the students and faculty. Often seen carrying the *Sporting News*, Father Kelly built a legacy of athletic enthusiasm at Bishop England High School. A stern disciplinarian, the rector gained great affection

The iconic bench statue of Monsignor Robert J. Kelly sits near the Father O'Brien Gymnasium in the BEHS courtyard. *Photo by author.*

from a generation of students. He assisted in the physical transition of the high school to Daniel Island in 1998. His religious attributes were always ingrained within his warmth of character. Though there exist records of baptisms and especially the sacrament of holy matrimony, the impressive demand of his officiate services by former students bears mention. He had the ability to be close to his flock, much like Doc O'Brien, to the point that his influence was both deep and wide.

His passing in 2004 did leave another legacy along with the iconic sculptured bronze bench posturing his image in the courtyard of the new school he visited often, especially during athletic contests. The baseball field is named for him. Father Kelly often brought out the best in his students, usually building long-term friendships that transcended the four years of growth the school inured. Quite the competitor, many a fine athlete in the 1960s and 1970s marveled at his considerable skills, abilities of mentorship and example of sportsmanship.

The sisters have served the community in nearly every aspect as well. We knew them by the first names of saints, whom they emulated, never really learning their last names. They taught us, healed us and inspired us. They were in evidence at our parochial schools, hospitals and, of course, Bishop England High School. They were unassuming yet essential personalities who advanced our grasp of

Father O'Brien reads to his nephews. *Courtesy of O'Brien family archives.*

Left: Bishop John England. *Courtesy of Archival Office of the Diocese of Charleston.*

Below: Bishop's quarters, 114 Broad Street, Charleston. The building was purchased in 1866 by Bishop P.N. Lynch and restored to its current state after devastation from the earthquake of 1886. The building dates from 1790. Bishop Robert E. Guglielmone, the thirteenth bishop of Charleston, has occupied the residence since 2009. *Photo by author.*

the world ahead of us. They were unforgettable religious women—such as Sister Margaretta, Sister Amelia, Sister Marie and Sister Mary Louise—with an abundance of preparation and energy for the challenge. There are so many more who have formed our little fingers around pencils, taught us the Catechism and brought the world to us through literature.

Where will Catholicity turn in the need for pastoral care? In the United States, the last fifty years show a startling reduction in seminarians, from 8,335 in 1965 to 3,631 in 2014.[94] In that same period, the United States has shown a significant drop in priests, from 58,632 to 38,275. Yet the worldwide population of priests has remained relatively static. Thus, there are more priests emigrating from other countries to fill the void of U.S.-born priests. The Catholic population has doubled in those same fifty years. There are nearly 1.25 billion Catholics worldwide, 75 million in the United States. Catholics represent 24 percent of the U.S. population.[95] There is a pronounced dearth of young women in service to the church as well. There were 179,954 sisters serving parishes, schools, hospitals, orphanages and communities in 1965. A Georgetown University study reported only 49,883 in 2014.[96] But unlike the priesthood, the last fifty years show nearly a 30 percent decline in the population of religious sisters worldwide.

Ostensibly, the responsibility falls upon the Catholic family. Lay service to the Catholic Church must continue to support the needs of the Catholic community, as well as Catholic charities that serve others well outside the Catholic sphere. These are seen today in the form of deacons, Eucharistic ministers, lay teachers, retired nurses and doctors who assist outreach missions and a plethora of other needs fulfilled by volunteers. Those needs remain profound.

In an ever-changing world, the call to assist or support by the assets of time, talent and treasure have become even more important. It is within the selfless legacy of John England, who walked the streets of Charleston without soles on his shoes, that the quiet act of self-sacrifice becomes part of the Catholic psyche. It is from the humble principles of Joseph Laurence O'Brien that we strive to elevate our next generation to the promise of learning and the fulfillment of greater understanding.

Bishop John England authored a prayer that is repeated daily by the order he founded, the Sisters of Charity of Our Lady of Mercy. With this prayer, we conclude.

Prayer of Bishop John England

Blessed Jesus,
I devote and consecrate myself this day
To your honor and service.
In whatsoever way
It shall please You to dispose of me.
Direct my superiors to point out that path
Whither You wish me to go,
And give me the grace to obey.
Holy Virgin, Mother of my Savior,
I place myself
Under your special patronage,
Obtain for me from your Son
All the graces
Which my weakness stands in need of.
Protect me in life and
Defend me in death.
                                    Amen.

AFTERWORD

The study of two righteous priests within the quilt of their times has gained timeless relevance. They have taught us principles that apply whether one is sixteen or sixty-two. They have welcomed the ordeal in order to facilitate the ideal.

Science continues to seek the mysteries of life, to improve health and to discover ways in which humankind can exceed age barriers. Everyone wants to live longer. What we have learned from the lives of Bishop England and Monsignor O'Brien is that living a long life should never be the goal. One should seek to live the wide and selfless life.

In living selflessly wide, there is an inherent opportunity to better serve mankind. England and O'Brien expanded their spheres to enjoy spiritual significance in all relationships and in all peoples. The broadened life is one that has no fear, no bias and no perimeter. There is a unique enthusiasm—a passion—in committing oneself to the sincere and humble service of others. Selflessness is, perhaps, the highest estate one may obtain in the comportment of life. It rises above the earthly values of property, gemstones and the trappings of wealth. There is a biblical quality in living purposely beyond the fruits of abundance and the temptation of self-aggrandizement.

The world we live in promotes the opposite: the inherited attainment of privilege. Within affluence, material things are bestowed, maintained and admired. Generational families are often torn apart by the reading of a will or the value of an old portrait. These things matter not.

Bishop Guglielmone gives a blessing to BEHS students, 2012. *Courtesy of BEHS Archives.*

Daughters, barely of driving age, want a new sports car; sons demand the latest Play Station or cellphone. These are false necessities, though the rationalization of such portends otherwise. When earthly things exceed the connection of a meaningful relationship, our societal values become skewed. Yet we tend to judge privilege and pretension with astigmatic vision. So much that we deem to be essential is simply a deceptive appraisal of reality. Living wide corrects our vision.

In the study of the two holy priests, we discover that their enthusiasm of life was passed on to others. It became infectious. Those who they met and befriended likely gained an equal enthusiasm for them and what they represented. No doubt, many who crossed paths with these selfless and humble men were inspired to "live wider" within their own lives. It is not enough, as is ascribed herein, to say, "live selflessly, live wide." One must wholeheartedly commit and perform all aspects of this higher aspiration. Spontaneous and anonymous givers are the best illustration of this attitude.

Bishop John England came to Charleston committed to perform, despite the overwhelming risks of poor funding, non-acceptance and ultimately declining health. Father Joseph Laurence O'Brien came under another set of impossible circumstances: hesitant bias, a world war and a long cycle of economic difficulties. Yet both persevered. What they founded is still here in the form of organizational precepts, religious community and educational institutions. They rose from being important stewards of their times to a much more elevated plateau of being studied as exemplary and significant figures for times beyond.

It is all the more inspiring that the paths they took had so many impediments yet so many glorious vistas and warming campfires. Indeed, their early kindling of Catholicity can be felt today in every homily, every sacrament and every fingertip extended into the holy waters of our next blessing.

NOTES

INTRODUCTION

1. Carlow College. www.carlowcollege.ie.

CHAPTER 1

2. George M. Stephens, "John Locke: His American and Carolinian Legacy," John Locke Foundation. johnlocke.org/about/who_is_john_locke_essay.html.
3. "Irish Rebellion and John England," *Journal of the American Irish Historical Society* 14 (n.d.): 116.

CHAPTER 2

4. New Advent, "John England." www.newadvent.org/cathen/05470a.htm.
5. Thomas Bartlett, "The 1798 Irish Rebellion," BBC History. www.bbc.co.uk/history/british/empire_seapower/irish_reb_01.shtml.
6. Jonathan Clark, "The American Revolution: A War of Religion?" HistoryToday. www.historytoday.com/jonathan-clark/american-revolution-war-religion.
7. Agatha Aimar Simmons, *Brief History of St. Mary's Roman Catholic Church* (Charleston, SC: J.J. Furlong & Co., 1961), 10.
8. Ibid., 18.
9. Ibid.
10. Sister Anne Francis Campbell, OLM, "Bishop England's Sisterhood, 1829–1929," written dissertation, 1968, 3.
11. Joseph Lawrence O'Brien, *John England, Bishop of Charleston: Apostle to Democracy* (New York: Edward O'Toole, 1934).

12. Cyclopaedia.net, "John England (bishop)," www.cyclopaedia.de/wiki/John_England_(bishop).

13. Dr. Peter Guilday, ed., *The Life and Times of John England, 1786–1842*, vol. 1 (n.p.: American Press, 1927).

14. Wikipedia, "Largest Cities in the U.S. by Population by Decade," en.wikipedia.org/wiki/Largest_cities_in_the_United_States_by_population_by_decade#1790.

CHAPTER 3

15. Catholic Diocese of Charleston Archives, "Inventory of the Bishop John England Correspondence, 1820–1839," www.catholic-doc.org/ac/?p=collections/findingaid&id=147&q=&rootcontentid=9087.

16. New Advent, "Penal Laws," www.newadvent.org/cathen/11611c.htm.

17. Diocese of Cork & Ross, "Most Rev. John England," www.corkandross.org/priests.jsp?priestID=397.

18. Joseph Kelly, "Charleston's Bishop John England and American Slavery," Project Muse, muse.jhu.edu/login?auth=0&type=summary&url=/journals/new_hibernia_review/v005/5.4kelly.html.

18. Ibid.

20. Catholic Diocese of Charleston Archives, "Inventory of the Bishop John England Correspondence."

21. Diocese of Cork & Ross, "Most Rev. John England."

22. Encyclopedia Britannica, "John England," www.britannica.com/EBchecked/topic/187865/John-England.

23. New Advent, "John England."

24. New Advent, "Daniel O'Connell," www.newadvent.org/cathen/11200c.htm.

CHAPTER 4

25. Roman Catholic Diocese of Charleston, "Black Catholic History," www.sccatholic.org/african-american-ministry/black-catholic-history.

26. University College Cork, "Irish Emigration History," www.ucc.ie/en/emigre/history.

27. Kelly, "Charleston's Bishop John England."

28. Roman Catholic Diocese of Charleston, "Black Catholic History."

29. Guilday, *Life and Times of John England*, 76–77.

30. Ibid.

31. Ibid.

32. Gale, "Southern Literary Messenger," gdc.gale.com/archivesunbound/archives-unbound-the-southern-literary-messenger-literature-of-the-old-south.

33. United States History, "Nullification Crisis," www.u-s-history.com/pages/h333.html.

34. Guilday, *Life and Times of John England*, 20.

35. Joseph Esposito, "The First Catholic Voice before Congress," *National Catholic Register*, August 30, 1998, www.ncregister.com/site/article/the_first_catholic_voice_before_congress.

36. Ibid.

37. Ibid.

38. Ibid.

39. Rita H. DeLorme, "Bishop John England's 'Haytian Legation': Failure or Success?" *Southern Cross*, February 3, 2011. diosav.org/sites/all/files/archives/9105p05.pdf.

40. Guilday, *Life and Times of John England*.

41. DeLorme, "Bishop John England's 'Haytian Legation.'"

42. Sacred Congregation of Propaganda is an administration of the Vatican responsible for the spread of Catholicism. New Advent, "Sacred Congregation of Propaganda," www.newadvent.org/cathen/12456a.htm.

43. Ibid.

44. John England, *The Works of the Right Reverend John England, First Bishop of Charleston*, books.google.com/books?id=4nJLAAAAMAAJ&pg=PA24&lpg=PA24&dq=funeral+of+Bishop+John+england&source=bl&ots=Gm_nS0MVTe&sig=sGzRqilJtT_Ihr21kr Xl7ozJemg&hl=en&sa=X&ei=UHUDVNiCB8aPNo6NgJgN&ved=0CDIQ6AEw Aw#v=onepage&q=funeral%20of%20Bishop%20John%20england&f=false.

45. New Advent, "John England."

46. Rita H. DeLorme, "Focusing on Bishop John England of Charleston as Author, Editor and Visionary," *Southern Cross*, February 19, 2004, diosav.org/sites/all/files/archives/S8408p03_0.pdf.

47. Esposito, "First Catholic Voice before Congress."

CHAPTER 5

48. O'Brien, *John England*.

49. Ben M. Bogard, "Richard Fuller, DD," Baptist History Homepage, baptisthistoryhomepage.com/fuller.richard.by.bogard.html.

CHAPTER 6

50. Leonard Swidler, "St. John Carroll and St. John England, Democratic Saints," Association for the Rights of Catholics in the Church, www.arcc-catholic-rights.net/HISTORICAL%20BACKGROUND.htm.

51. Ibid.

52. Ibid.

53. Ibid.

CHAPTER 7

54. New Advent, "Diocese of Scranton," www.newadvent.org/cathen/13633a.htm.

55. Catholic Diocese of Charleston Archives, "Mary Shahid Papers, 1938, 1952," www.catholic-doc.org/archive1/?p=collections/findingaid&id=130&q=&rootc ontentid=57172.

56. Ibid.

57. Georgina Pell Curtis and Benedict Elder, eds., *The American Catholic Who's Who*, "O'Brien, Rt. Rev. Joseph Laurence," http://books.google.com/ books?id=lr0SAAAAIAAJ&pg=PA337&lpg=PA337&dq=Monsignor+Joseph+ L.+O'Brien&source=bl&ots=63lsaiUZFC&sig=Ut31qvdkEEzJrwYP5n0AFMv F3s4&hl=en&sa=X&ei=-nIEVJD2Oc_JgwTq8oIg&ved=0CDoQ6AEwBTgK #v=onepage&q=Monsignor%20Joseph%20L.%20O'Brien&f=false.

58. Catholic Diocese of Charleston Archives, "Mary Shahid Papers."

59. Curtis and Elder, *American Catholic Who's Who*, "O'Brien, Rt. Rev. Joseph Laurence."

60. Catholic Diocese of Charleston Archives, "Mary Shahid Papers."

61. Information gathered from the Archives of the Sisters of Charity of Our Lady of Mercy at May Forest.

62. This notable Charleston-based architect designed the building at Hampstead Square circa 1904.

63. O'Brien Family Papers, letter to Bishop Northrup.

64. Private Papers of Monsignor Joseph Lawrence O'Brien, unpublished. Diocesan Office of Archives, 41.

65. Monsignor J.L. O'Brien pamphlet.

66. Bourke Cockran, circular letter from Reverend J.L. O'Brien to Catholic community, archives of the Diocese of Charleston.

67. Ibid.

68. Biographical Directory of the United States Congress, "COCKRAN, William Bourke (1854–1923)," bioguide.congress.gov/scripts/biodisplay. pl?index=C000575.

69. "Talking Motion Pictures," xroads.virginia.edu/~UG00/3on1/movies/talkies. html.

70. Passage taken from the notes and letters of Reverend Monsignor Joseph Lawrence O'Brien. Times and methods preened from *Pittsburgh Press*, "Dancing in 1917 Will Be a Jazz Mania and the Dance Craze Crazier Than Ever," September 10, 1917, news.google.com/newspapers?nid=1144&dat=19170910&id=s0UbAAA AIBAJ&sjid=aUkEAAAAIBAJ&pg=2346,3160934.

71. Circular letter copy from Reverend J.L. O'Brien, archives of the Diocese of Charleston.

72. Correspondence of Reverend J.L. O'Brien, archives of the Diocese of Charleston.

73. Ibid.

74. O'Brien family archives of 2014, donated to the Diocese of Charleston.

75. "In Memoriam: The Right Reverend Monsignor James J. May 1887–1958." From the *Catholic Miscellany*, 1958. Courtesy of May Forest Motherhouse Archives.

76. Notes from the correspondence of Reverend J.L. O'Brien, archives of the Diocese of Charleston.

77. Ibid.

78. Ibid.

79. Papers of Reverend J.L. O'Brien, archives of the Diocese of Charleston.

80. Correspondence of Reverend J.L. O'Brien, archives of the Diocese of Charleston.

81. Ibid.

82. Curtis and Elder, *American Catholic Who's Who*, "O'Brien, Rt. Rev. Joseph Laurence."

CHAPTER 8

83. Guilday, *Life and Times of John England*, 76–77.

84. *Southern Cross*, January 28, 1939, scr.stparchive.com/Archive/SCR/SCR01281939P21.php.

CHAPTER 9

85. New Advent, "John England."

86. Dana Lorelle, "Catholicism in the South: Once a Strange Religion, Now Forging Ahead with Evangelical Fervor," *National Catholic Register*, July 2, 2012, www.ncregister.com/daily-news/catholicism-in-the-south-once-a-strange-religion-now-forging-ahead-with-eva

87. Swidler, "St. John Carroll and St. John England."

CHAPTER 10

88. Ibid.

89. Ibid.

CHAPTER 11

90. O'Brien family archives of 2014, donated to the Diocese of Charleston.

91. Bishop England High School. "Athletics," www.behs.com/apps/pages/index.jsp?uREC_ID=171694&type=d&termREC_ID=&pREC_ID=352494.

92. Great Schools, "Bishop England High School," www.greatschools.org/south-carolina/charleston/1121-Bishop-England-High-School.

CHAPTER 12

93. Meadowlark Lemon. www.meadowlarklemon.org/biography.

94. CARA, "Frequently Requested Church Statistics," cara.georgetown.edu/caraservices/requestedchurchstats.html

95. Wikipedia, "Catholic Church by Country," en.wikipedia.org/wiki/Catholic_Church_by_country.

96. CARA, "Frequently Requested Church Statistics."

INDEX

ABOUT THE AUTHOR

W. Thomas McQueeney is a native of Charleston and the author of two other books, *The Rise of Charleston* (2011) and *Sunsets Over Charleston* (2012). He is a 1974 graduate of The Citadel (BA English) and has served on St. Francis Xavier Hospital Board, The Citadel Board of Visitors, the MUSC Children's Hospital Board, the Patriot's

Courtesy of Katie M. Altman.

Point Maritime Museum Board and The Citadel Foundation Board. He chaired the $44.5 million revitalization of Johnson Hagood Stadium (2003–8) and the Southern Conference Basketball Championships. He is the founder and chairman of the Medal of Honor Bowl. A local businessman, he received the Order of the Palmetto in 2009, the highest award bestowed upon a citizen of the state of South Carolina. As a student at Bishop England High School (class of 1970), he was a four-sport letterman, class president, football captain and honor graduate.

....
Visit us at
www.historypress.net
....